WAR STORIES

Behind the Silver and Gold Shields

By
Dr. Thomas J. Ward
Director of the Criminal Justice Program
St. John's University
Jamaica, New York

Foreword by
Bernard B. Kerik, New York City
Police Commissioner (Ret.)

43-08 162nd Street
Flushing, NY 11358
www.LooseleafLaw.com   800-647-5547

Library of Congress Cataloging-in-Publication Data

Ward, Thomas J., 1948-
    War stories : behind the silver and gold shields / by Thomas J. Ward ; foreword by Bernard B. Kerik.
        p. cm.
    ISBN 1-889031-58-5
    1. Ward, Thomas J., 1948- 2. Police--New York (State)--New York--Biography. 2. Criminal justice personnel--New York (State)--New York--Biography. I. Title.
        HV7911.W33 W3 2002
        364.92--dc21

2002006478

Cover design by: Armen Edgarian
                  armenjohn@aol.com

Shields on front cover are those
actually worn by Thomas Ward.

Dedication

This book is dedicated to my wife, Patricia, and our son, Tom, for their unwavering support and love through the years. Without them, I could not have survived the trials and tribulations of life. All my great joy in life flows from their untiring love and loyalty.

Special thanks go to my daughter-in-law, Janet and to my granddaughter Emma, the gorgeous little redhead who has wrapped me around her finger—and I love every minute of it. Janet and Emma have added so much to my already wonderful life.

And to Thomas and Evelyn Ward, my parents, who taught me right from wrong. I hope I have not let you down. And to Cecilia Staudt, my maternal grandmother, who taught me never, ever to give up.

And to the criminal justice personnel of America who every day strive to preserve our freedom and protect our rights, you remain my real heroes.

And to the future protectors of America, I wish you safe passage through life.

Acknowledgments

T here are so many people I would like to thank for their support of this effort. My dear friends, Ed and Evelyn DeBlasio, Bob and Joan Finck, Jay and Cheryl Minsky, George and Ellie Olivet, and Ronnie and Pam Risch, all of whom encouraged me to write my story and share it with the next generation of criminal justice practitioners. You prodded me to bang the keys and flesh out my story. More important, your friendship and love are gifts I cherish.

I feel a special debt of gratitude to my colleagues and good friends at St. John's University: Professor Peter P. Cardalena, Jr. who reviewed the manuscript from cover to cover and offered constructive and welcomed comments, and to Dr. Karim Ismaili who also insisted that this work was publishable. I also want to thank Dr. Frank Straub, the former Deputy Commissioner for Training with the NYPD, who supported me throughout this endeavor.

To my colleague, Professor John McCabe – "The Chief" – who has demonstrated an untiring and selfless commitment to serving our students while battling a trying illness, I thank you for being an inspiration to all of us.

To the men and women of New York's Finest and New York's Boldest, I thank you for all you do to make our communities and jails safer. The remarkable work of the NYPD and the unheralded story of the New York City Department of Correction inspire me every day. I salute my former colleagues for their courage and devotion to duty.

I particularly want to thank those who I had the privilege of serving with in the NYPD's Tactical Patrol Force. As the saying goes about TPF, "Their like will not be seen again."

I cannot forget those dedicated professors whose guidance and inspiration helped me navigate through my life's *War Stories*. To my students who constantly inspire me and leave me convinced that teaching is a noble and rewarding profession, I am eternally grateful.

I shall never forget Professor Leo C. Loughrey, the late Chairman of the Division of Law and Police Science at John Jay College of Criminal Justice, who gave me my first opportunity to teach and started me on my journey in higher education. I will always be indebted to Dr. Alexander B. Smith, my criminology professor at John Jay College of Criminal Justice, who today remains my dear friend and mentor. And to my good friends, Bob and Debbie Jackson, and David and Kerry Rice, my former students at the State University at Utica/Rome who still keep in touch with their old professor and make me feel proud to know such good and decent people.

I would be remiss if I did not mention Herman and Dorothy Fluegge, our wonderful friends and neighbors, who I know would be delighted to see in print the stories they heard for so many years. Dotty and Herman were among the first to convince me that my tale should be committed to writing. May these good souls rest in peace.

To the members of The Gourmet Club—Jack and Delia Gray, Richie and Carol Rossi, Bill and Susan Emery and wannabe members Dave and Chris Pascale, I am grateful for all you taught me about humor and loyal friendship over the years.

To my father-in-law, John Marsling, who has always stood by me in all my endeavors, I hold dear your loyalty and inexhaustible support over the years.

To my brother-in-law, Dan Marsling and his wife Antoinette, and my sister-in-law Kathy Hom and her husband Stan, I treasure your unwavering support.

Last but certainly not least, I am forever grateful to Tom Creelman who has been with me through thick and thin and is the one guy I want in the foxhole with me during the proverbial "call to arms."

To all of you, I owe a great debt of gratitude.

Table of Contents

About the Author

D r. Thomas J. Ward is an Associate Professor and Director of the Criminal Justice Program at St. John's University, where he founded the graduate program in *Criminal Justice Leadership*.

Before joining the faculty at St. John's University, he served as Assistant Commissioner for Training and Organizational Development at the New York City Department of Correction—the nation's largest jail system—where he was the recipient of the agency's *Distinguished Service Award for Leadership.*

Dr. Ward began his criminal justice career as a member of the New York City Police Department, where he served in the elite Tactical Patrol Force and in the Detective Division as both an undercover operative and as an investigator. He has also held senior executive positions in security administration and earned a national reputation as an expert on health care fraud.

Dr. Ward holds Bachelor of Science and Master of Arts degrees from John Jay College of Criminal Justice and a Doctorate in Public Administration (D.P.A.) from Nova Southeastern University.

He serves as Chairman of the New York City Police Commissioner's Board of Visitors and as a member of the Police Advisory Committee for Nassau County, New York. Dr. Ward is also a member of the Board of Trustees of the New York Correction History Society, and he serves as a consultant to the National Institute of Justice.

Dr. Ward was raised in Brooklyn, New York and now lives on Long Island with his wife, Patricia.

Foreword

I was pleased when Dr. Tom Ward asked me to write this Foreword because I consider Tom a good friend, a loyal colleague and a valued advisor. In *War Stories,* Tom has written a superb book filled with thoughtful insights about many of the challenges facing the criminal justice system.

Tom's diverse career as a criminal justice practitioner began as a member of the famed Tactical Patrol Force of the New York City Police Department and culminated with his appointment as Assistant Commissioner for Training and Organizational Development at the New York City Department of Correction. Tom and I share the special honor and bond of having served in both of these outstanding law enforcement agencies.

There are very few criminal justice leaders who have traveled the path that Tom Ward has journeyed, and far fewer individuals who can write a story as artfully as Tom does in *War Stories.* By writing instructive and entertaining accounts of his experiences as a police officer, corrections executive and college professor, Tom captivates the readers. Tom Ward is a gifted storyteller, and readers will discover that he has seamlessly and skillfully penned his life's story and subtly laced it with wise and humble counsel.

Tom Ward is a gentleman and scholar, so I am delighted to introduce the fascinating life story of my friend and distinguished colleague.

Bernard B. Kerik
NYC Police Commissioner (Ret.)
& NYC Correction Commissioner (Ret.)

Preface

In writing *War Stories*, I revisited my professional life and unveiled some segments of my personal life because there is a nexus between the two. For when you serve in the criminal justice system, you are essentially choosing a *way of life* that will affect your mind, body, heart and soul—as well as your loved ones. Criminal Justice is a field where the personal and the professional can either harmonize or clash.

My unorthodox career path has provided me with numerous experiences and anecdotes, which I believe can be instructive for those who wish to serve in the criminal justice system and for those readers who just want to learn more about crime and justice.

This is not a traditional textbook by any stretch of the imagination—and there are no lectures reprinted on the following pages. But I believe that there are important lessons to be culled from my "adventures" over the last three decades, as I journeyed from college dropout to becoming—as I describe myself—a "blue-collar" professor.

War Stories introduces a new *genre* to criminal justice literature, one that employs a candid and introspective biography, to highlight some of the most pressing issues facing the criminal justice system in the 21st Century.

War Stories is not fiction, and the dialogue and prose are unvarnished at times to capture the reality of the "street" or milieu.

War Stories describes my journey through life; it certainly is not intended to be a primer describing how students and criminal justice practitioners or anyone else should live their lives. Should someone learn something from my mistakes or benefit from my experiences, then burning the midnight oil and revisiting the past will have been all worth it.

Thomas J. Ward

Chapter 1
The Paradise Bar & Grill

T he shrill ring of the phone pierced the night's stillness and instantly angered me, for I knew it was the police informing my dad that his small and unprofitable bar, located on the Brooklyn waterfront, had been burglarized again.

I got up from bed and watched my dad get dressed as my mother instructed me to go back to bed, telling me—as usual—that everything would be all right.

But this time I would get dressed and go with my dad, who looked so disheartened and defeated. My mother reluctantly consented to let me accompany my dad, so I threw on my dungarees and my blue Dodgers jacket and joined my father for the six-block ride to *The Paradise Bar & Grill*. Jerry the cop just shook his head and pointed to the broken plate glass strewn all over the sidewalk. The newly delivered stock of liquor, paid for with borrowed money, was all gone.

I started to sob and thought, "why does this always happen to us? Why couldn't my dad be like everyone else and just work a job where he would be home for dinner and not have to worry about criminals wrecking his bar and stealing his liquor?"

I hid my tears from my dad who didn't need to see this at this time. Besides, I wanted to go with him the next time the cops called and didn't want him to think his 10-year-old was weak and not up to the task. The cops would call many times during my youth, and numerous times I would escort my dad to another crime scene where detectives would search for fingerprints and just shake their heads in despair. I learned to hold my tears until I returned to bed for another night of tossing and turning. My dad had fought against the Japanese in World War II and had come home victorious. How come we were now losing this battle to some punks just six blocks from where we lived? For years, I prayed every day that the burglars would get caught or would just stop, but it seemed the Lord had His hands full dealing with other matters, so the nighttime calls continued.

Some years later, the police would discover that a burglar had viciously assaulted our beloved watchdog, ironically named *Lucky*. The lovable mongrel had put up a heroic fight, but had been hit across his head by a two-by-four that was found near his almost lifeless body. *Lucky's* left eye had been dislodged from its socket. *Lucky* would be rushed to an ASPCA hospital in Manhattan where, after hours of surgery, he would be saved. The incident would receive widespread media coverage that resulted in my dad receiving telegrams and letters from as far away as California wishing the hero dog a quick recovery. *Lucky* would receive the ASPCA's highest award and would return to live a long and healthy life in *The Paradise* he fought so hard to defend.

One week after the horrific assault on *Lucky*, the phone rang at 3:00 A.M. Now seventeen I no longer had to argue with my mother about going with my dad when we received these dreaded calls. But this time the message would be different. The police officer told my dad that there were burglars in the bar, but the front window had not been broken; they had probably entered from a rear door. The police, while on patrol, noticed some movement in the bar but decided to pass by and park the radio car, walking back to better observe the situation by peeking into the bar. The cops did not want to break the window to gain entrance because they knew my father didn't have insurance. My father and I jumped into his 1956 gray and white Buick and sped to an agreed upon location up the block from the bar. The cops asked my dad for his keys and my father said that it was difficult to engage the lock, and that it would be better if he would sneak up to the door and quickly open it for the cops. The two patrolmen agreed, and I was instructed to stay in the background where I would be safe. But once my father and the cops started moving toward the bar, I decided to trail closely behind.

My father turned the lock and charged right through the open door, followed by the stunned cops and me. My dad grabbed a tall, startled burglar and was all set to punch his lights out, when the guy screamed, "He hit the dog—not me," as he pointed to a table, where hiding under it, was another young punk. My father started to make his way toward the accomplice when the cops, guns now drawn, prevented him from going after the second thief. These were the same bastards who savagely beat *Lucky*.

I experienced an odd mix of emotions that morning, ranging from anger and disgust to a newly felt sense of adventure. There was even a sense of exhilaration, knowing that these criminals would now go to prison for their cowardly deeds. Finally, my prayers were answered—so I thought.

Both burglars had criminal records and pleaded guilty to some type of trespassing. They received 30 days in jail. There was no trial, no mention of the assault on *Lucky,* and no restitution. The appearance before the judge was nothing like I thought it would be, and my dad never had a chance to tell the judge what great harm these bums had done to our entire family. There was something wrong here; something that should not happen in America. This is not what was taught in high school about the American justice system; this had to be some kind of mistake or aberration, for the entire affair made absolutely no sense to a 17-year-old. This was not justice!

Chapter 2
Crime: Up Close and Personal

I suspect there are many reasons why someone decides to pursue a particular occupation or profession. Some of these motivations are clearly connected to life's experiences, while others are less discernible and perhaps more complicated. It took me decades to explore the reasons why I decided to become a New York City cop. But not until I started to write this book did I understand the motivation behind this decision and the forces that helped shape it.

I attended Our Lady of Perpetual Help grammar school in Bay Ridge, Brooklyn, during the 1950s when the primary focus of my existence from spring training through the long, hot summer was the Brooklyn Dodgers, and praying that they would eventually beat the hated Yankees in The World Series. Finally, in 1955, a fearless 23-year-old named Johnny Podres hurled a shutout against the Bronx Bombers and the Borough of Kings celebrated its first and only World Championship. I remember watching the last out in *The Paradise* as the bar's patrons—mostly longshoremen and seamen— erupted in cheers as my dad sounded a mariner's bell he had affixed to the wall just for that purpose. Finally, dad got to ring the bell.

Roger Kahn's eloquent account of the Dodgers, which he called *The Boys of Summer*, beautifully captured the passions and aspirations of Brooklyn's loyal working-class fans. The sounding of my dad's bell saluted the triumph of blue-collar Brooklyn over the perennial World Champions from the Bronx. There would be no "wait 'til next year" this time, as my dad announced that drinks were on the house. Liquor flowed for hours and this wonderful party is forever stored in my memory.

If the Dodgers were the focus of our collective affection, then the parish was the focal point of daily life. Every day began with Mass, and frequently I served as an altar boy, enchanted by the mysticism of the Holy Eucharist and the liturgical aspects of Holy Mother Church. For much of the time during grammar school, I had an abiding desire to become a Redemptorist priest. I had actually started the admissions process in the 8th grade, when I realized that I did not have a vocation to the celibate priesthood. As an only child, I don't think this realization broke my parents' hearts, as they certainly looked forward to a grandchild carrying forth the Ward name.

During the 6th grade I became a hallway monitor and school safety patrolman who proudly wore the silver shield engraved with the *AAA* logo of the American Automobile Association. I cannot tell you how much I enjoyed this assignment; for me it was a rite of passage, because I had always looked up to and envied the upper classmen who manned the hallways and the posts at the various intersections surrounding the school. Now I was one of them. The school safety patrol had an organizational hierarchy that started with patrolman and had promotional ranks of sergeant, lieutenant and captain. Different enamel paints in the center of the badges signified the monitor's rank. The center of the sergeant's shield was green, the lieutenant's badge sported red, and the captains had an eye-catching royal blue in the center of their silver shields. This quasi-military organizational design was fully accepted by the monitors, who were well respected, and could hand out written disciplinary or punishment assignments to those kids who had the temerity to disobey orders.

The job had power and prestige and this was further enhanced when Sister Cabrini took over and had us wear white gloves and powder blue garrison hats as part of our everyday uniform. We were to stand inspections to make sure that our shields were properly attached to the white safety belts, and that our gloves and hats were clean and properly worn. Sister Cabrini was General Patton in a Josephite habit and her demeanor filled kids with trepidation as she walked the halls to check the posts. All she was missing were the white pit bull and the pearl-handled sidearm.

On the long-awaited day that I thought I'd be promoted to sergeant, a bully I had had some encounters with over the years, decided to test my mettle by grabbing my bus pass and throwing it out the bus window as we headed to school. I had reached the end of the line with this jerk, so I hauled off and belted him in the jaw before getting off the bus to retrieve my pass. Well, the kid's face blew up and although I don't think he snitched on me, the ubiquitous Sister Cabrini got wind of the situation and decided that I was not worthy of promotion to sergeant. I thought my days as a monitor were numbered, but the situation cooled down and I was left with my silver shield—and a school yard reputation as someone with a temper not to fool with.

Maybe I got a fair deal, but I could never figure out why I wasn't promoted if the whole thing was not serious enough to warrant my dismissal from the monitors. Sister Cabrini never said a word to me, but she knew what happened, and I guess she cut me some slack by not throwing me off the monitors for beating the shit out of a bully. I guess she felt that the promotion would bring attention to the whole issue, so the best way to handle it would be to do nothing, and let the whole thing disappear. Actually, I think she secretly applauded the fact that I knocked the bully on his ass, but she didn't want to send a signal to the other kids that punching someone's lights out was an appropriate resolution to a problem. The momentary self-gratification cost me a promotion, but the bully never bothered anyone on the bus again. On balance, I guess the outcome wasn't that bad after all.

My dad bought me a shoeshine kit when I was about 10 years old, and I immediately went to work at *The Paradise* shining the shoes of military personnel from the Brooklyn Army Terminal, which was an expansive warehouse complex with four deep water piers that jutted into New York harbor. The Army Base—as we called it—was located directly across the street from the bar. The shoeshine money was good and I also picked up a few more bucks by sweeping the floor, cleaning the bathrooms, and filling the ice-filled cooler with long-necked bottles of Rheingold and Ballantine. I used the cash to buy baseball cards, which I flipped and traded at school.

I usually drove my 3-speed bike the six blocks from home to *The Paradise*. Occasionally, I would venture down to the bicycle path along the Belt Parkway, which ran parallel to the Narrows, where majestic-looking passenger liners—such as the Queen Elizabeth—would make their way into New York's busy harbor. One day Johnny Napoli and I were cruising along the path when I saw it all happening in front of me. We were about to get mugged, right out in the open on a bright sunny day in June! Johnny was in front of me, so it was now impossible for him to stop and make a sudden U-turn. A pack of four kids raced toward us and pushed us off our bikes; they then grabbed us and told us to empty our pockets, which we did.

I don't remember saying a word to these kids, who had to be about 13 or 14. Johnny and I were about three years younger than these kids, so I guess we appeared to be easy targets. I handed over my 63 cents and they released us with the warning that if we went to the cops they would get us.

We headed back to *The Paradise* and told my dad and Phil Mandel, a retired taxi driver who hung around the bar, what had happened. All four of us jumped in Phil's green Plymouth, which looked very much like an unmarked police car. Phil drove to the 69th Street Pier where we saw the four kid-robbers casting their fishing lines into the polluted Narrows. Phil grabbed two of the kids by their necks and my father grabbed the other two by their arms. The punks looked petrified. Phil took out a detective's badge and said that they were all going to jail. The wise-ass kids started to cry and begged Phil and my dad to release them; they promised they would never do anything like that again. Johnny and I took all of this in, and we were worried that these kids would follow through on their promise to get us if we went to the cops. They didn't know that Phil was impersonating a cop, and I had no idea he was going to flash a police shield and scare the shit out of these juvenile delinquents. Anyway, Phil and my dad played it out and told the kids that if they ever go near Johnny and me again they would have their asses hauled off to jail. Phil towered over these kids and he made sure to grab the ringleader by the collar before telling all of them to get lost and stay clear of the bicycle path.

It took me well over a year before I returned to the bicycle path, and I never saw a glimpse of those kids again. I doubt, however, that we were this wolf pack's last victims. Johnny and I got our money back and with our skinned knees and bruised egos we went back to *The Paradise* where dad bought us meatball heroes, which we washed down with Cokes.

I always wondered where Phil got that gold detective's badge; I never asked him about it. I don't know if Phil would have made a good cop, but he was a damn good actor and a real police buff.

═══════════════════════

One day I was working at *The Paradise* when a burly, sloppy-looking police sergeant sauntered into the bar and headed directly to the men's room. A few minutes later he came out and walked over to my grandmother who was tending bar and said that he was going to issue her a summons. My grandmother wanted to know why. The sergeant told her that there had been no soap in the bathroom and that was a violation. He started to pull out his summons book when my grandmother came barreling toward him, with her finger pointed at the stunned sergeant. And she didn't stop there. She took him by the arm and started pushing him toward the door. The noisy bar suddenly became dead silent, as the longshoremen and armed forces personnel watched to see if this sergeant would do something foolish to my grandmother, who was steaming mad. She told the sergeant that if he ever came back in the bar looking for a handout, that it would be something he would regret his entire life. She also mentioned the precinct commander's name, and you could see that this caught the sergeant's attention. The red-faced shakedown artist put his tail between his legs and scampered out of the bar like a scared rat. The bar erupted into cheers and my grandmother gave me a big wink, for she knew that I had just put a new bar of soap in the men's room; that was part of my job and I had done it just moments before this bum entered *The Paradise*. The sleazy sergeant had evidently flushed the soap down the toilet, and probably had done this many times before at other bars, before someone decided to confront him.

From this event, I learned early on how some corrupt cops would prey on innocent people and demean themselves and tarnish their shields. Fortunately, we never again saw that criminal parading around as a police sergeant. Rumor had it that he had been drummed out of the corps when caught red-handed in another corrupt act.

———————————

I also delivered newspapers after school and signed up for two routes: one was a weekly, *The Tablet,* and the other was a daily, *The Journal American*, which I delivered right after school. I quit the Journal route after a few months because kids would try to steal my bike as I climbed the stairs of apartment buildings to deliver the newspapers. I kept *The Tablet* route, which was a weekly paper published by the Catholic Diocese of Brooklyn. *The Tablet* cost 10 cents a week and the route was right in the neighborhood where I lived, so the whole job could be completed in an hour and a half.

One humid, terribly uncomfortable day in midsummer I started my route with my canvas bag stocked with the newspapers. I carried the bag over my shoulder and walked my route in order to avoid problems with any kids who wanted to steal my 3-speed racer. Across the street from our house on 63rd street lived a family whose 7-year-old daughter actually coaxed her mother into subscribing to the newspaper when I first came around trying to sell subscriptions. The little girl was a beautiful blonde with a sweet disposition; her mother was a genuinely nice person who, every week, gave me a dollar for the dime paper and told me to keep the change.

Their apartment would be my first stop of the day. I climbed the three stories to the nice lady's apartment and rang the bell. No answer. I tried again and waited, but again no answer. I descended two flights of stairs when I heard a door open and a man with a gravelly voice shout, "Yeah, what d'ya want?" I started to go back upstairs when it hit me that it would be better to wait and come back when the lady was there, for this way I would get my 90 cents tip. As I walked down the final staircase, I heard the door slam upstairs.

The next day cops were all over my block. Neighbors were outside their homes and uniformed cops and detectives seemed to be everywhere. I quickly got dressed and headed across the street where the center of the action seemed to be.

A neighbor pointed me out to the cops and I felt my heart pound against my chest. The detective asked me when was the last time I saw the lady on the third floor, the kind lady who obviously did not have a lot of money but insisted that I take a dollar from her every week. I told the detective I saw her last week. Then I told him what had happened yesterday.

I wondered why the cops were walking around with their pants rolled way up from their shoes. A little later two men carried a body bag from the building where the nice lady lived and put it in an old dirty van. Neighbors gasped and some cried, and I knew right away that the generous lady was dead. In fact, she had been murdered by her alcoholic husband, the same guy who had answered the door the day before. He had killed her with a shotgun a week before and kept her body in bed with him. Maggots were all over the bedroom and that's why the cops rolled up their pants; they didn't want the maggots to get into their trouser cuffs.

Neighbors had been troubled by the terrible smell emanating from the apartment and so they called the cops. Thank God the little girl had been away on vacation with relatives when this occurred. I never saw that little girl again, and I sometimes wonder what ever happened to her. It was said that her dad accused her mother of having an affair, a term I had never heard until that day and one I did not understand at the time.

I could not fathom why anyone would want to hurt that wonderful woman. And I never again delivered another newspaper.

Before we moved to 63rd Street, we lived on the fourth floor of an apartment building on 59th Street—just a block away from *The Paradise*. My father got together a down payment on a one-family house and we made the move into our new $17,500 home. It was said in my family that my father hit the number and that was the source of the down payment. It's probably true because my dad liked the ponies, and I know he bet on the Dodgers—quite heavily at times. Gambling was a constant source of friction in my family and it is probably the reason I dislike gambling so much and have no idea how to play cards or any other game of chance. Gambling made me very nervous as a kid because there were times when I know we didn't have the money to pay our bills. As an only child, it didn't affect me materially, for I always seemed to have more toys than my friends did. Actually, I had more toys than friends. But the gambling affected me emotionally, because I knew early on that my dad had a problem, which I am proud to say he conquered well before his untimely death from lung cancer, at the early age of 55.

One of the reasons we moved from 59th Street had to do with an incident that my grandmother witnessed one day as she returned from *The Paradise*, where she worked as a short-order cook and morning barmaid. My maternal grandmother was a tough piece of work—as tough as nails yet sublimely feminine. This day as she approached my apartment building a blast occurred that literally made her ears ring. Stunned by the boom, she turned and saw what she thought was a blanket rolling in the street, later to learn that it was a man blown from a car by a pipe bomb. Till this day, I still don't know what exactly happened, but the rumor again was that it had to do with jealousy, with the solution to someone's rage being a bomb. Later in the day I saw the car—or what remained of it—and then my grandparents whisked me away to their apartment, which was about a half-mile away. I spent quite a few days with my grandparents after this, and I know we all slept better knowing there were no bombs going off on their block. Shortly after the bombing we moved to our new home, which was only five blocks away—yet we felt it was in an entirely different neighborhood, a safer and more secure one.

During the 1950s families in Brooklyn generally stayed put and a move of just five blocks would be perceived as upward mobility. In our case, that's exactly what it was as we moved to our own home with a garage and three bedrooms and a little yard for a dog to play in. We moved to a new block with no bombs but where a crazed and alcoholic husband would kill his wife, the mother of his beautiful child. This was well before domestic violence became its own crime typology.

When I was a kid, I liked to read books about submarines. When that alarm sounded and the crew manned their stations, I could feel the excitement as the sleek sub pierced the cold and gray sea. The whole thing seemed romantic, and I became fascinated with the mysteries and the solitude of the sea.

My perception of the sea was radically altered when I realized that I was claustrophobic and that the sub dived to perilous depths to avoid the enemy's depth charges, which aimed to disintegrate the boat and kill its gallant sailors. Over time, I learned that even in books you cannot always escape from the harsh realities of life, that you can run but you really can't hide—that the descent to deeper and safer waters—and the flight to greener pastures—may be illusory.

Chapter 3
NYPD

T he police entrance exam took place on a brutally cold Saturday morning at Thomas Jefferson High School in Brooklyn, where thousands of young men stood in line to become one of New York's Finest. I was nineteen years old and convinced that I wanted a career in law enforcement. I had reviewed the study guides and felt confident that I had aced this civil service exam.

A few months later I rolled in at 3:00 A.M., after a night of partying, to find my mother awaiting me with a look that meant that I was in deep shit. She just stood there and waved a sheet of paper in her hand. It was a letter that indicated that I was to appear for the police physical in four hours; I had completely forgotten about the test. I jumped in the shower and then headed off to Thomas Street in lower Manhattan, where I joined hundreds of other guys who looked a helluva lot better than I did. After a battery of tests, which included pull-ups, sit-ups, curls with dumbbells and scaling over a 6-foot wooden wall after a short sprint, I cleared another hurdle on my way to becoming a cop—thanks to my mother.

On April 17, 1968, I reported to Police Headquarters at 240 Centre Street in lower Manhattan and was sworn in as a Police Trainee. At the time, I was a junior at John Jay College of Criminal Justice in Manhattan majoring in criminology, but I decided that this was the right time for me to join the force. During the 1960s and 1970s, the NYPD had a program that enabled young men between the ages of 17 and 20 to join the depart-ment as Trainees. Police Trainees would be assigned to various clerical assignments in precincts and other commands and then after graduating from the Police Academy they would be sworn in as Probationary Patrolmen upon reaching their 21st birthday. I was assigned to the Personnel Testing Unit in the Police Academy, which was the office that administered I.Q. tests to recruits and to police officers seeking assignments to the plainclothes and detective divisions.

My road to the Police Academy actually began at St. John's University in 1965 when I was a freshman majoring in history, with the goal to become a teacher and coach at the high school level. I was 17 years old and clearly not ready for higher education. All I wanted to do was play sports and party and sleep. I was a backup quarterback on the football team, which was actually a club sport that year, and I made the freshman baseball team as a slick fielding infielder. I was the last kid cut from the freshman basketball team, which was the team I really wanted to make. Except for a terrific throwing arm I had little natural athletic ability, but I worked harder than the next guy and had good instincts on the field and on the court.

Right away I dug myself into a hole at St. John's. I cut classes, failed to keep up with my readings and started to panic at mid-term time. I was simply too immature and undisciplined for the freedom afforded college kids. I hung around the gym in Alumni Hall and shot hoops during the day; at night I'd hit the local hangouts where I'd down a few beers with the guys from the football team. No one saw fit to ask a 17-year-old for proof.

Driving to the campus one day I saw a rookie cop directing traffic and right away that struck me as something I might like to do—not direct traffic but be a cop. The young rookie looked carefree; he looked like he was having a ball and he surely didn't look like he was concerned about philosophy, math and bio classes. The seed of interest in police work germinated at that intersection on Union Turnpike.

Fed up with college, I dropped out and considered joining the Marine Corps for a two-year enlistment, to be followed by a reserve commitment. But my father would not sign the permission papers and I needed his signature because I was only 17. I saw tears well up in his eyes as he started to tell me for the first time stories about his war experiences, so I told him I would wait awhile before finally deciding. In the meantime, my dad got me a job as a laborer unloading trucks at the Brooklyn Army Terminal, where I started to read library books, during my lunch break, about policing. The idea of using brawn the rest of my life hastened my decision to return to the books. The money wasn't bad, but the loading dock was not in my life's plans.

I visited my former guidance counselor at Xaverian High School who told me about a new college that prepared students for careers in law enforcement. It was called the College of Police Science and was part of the City University of New York. Better yet, it was located right in the New York City Police Academy on East 20th Street in Manhattan. I made a deal with myself: I would return to college and be serious about the books this time. I made a promise to myself that I would not blow this second chance.

I transferred to my new college, which shortly thereafter became John Jay College of Criminal Justice. This was a good match for me, even though I liked St. John's and felt guilty about dropping out in the middle of the spring semester. I felt I had let my parents down and I had exposed myself to the draft, as the war in Vietnam was raging and taking the lives of some of my former grade school and high school classmates.

I kept the laborer's job until I enrolled at John Jay in September of 1966. During the period I was working as a laborer and not in school, I did not get called for the draft even though I had exposed myself to it by giving up my college deferment. Now that I was back in school my college deferment would be reinstated. Shortly after re-enrolling in college our nation would move to a lottery system, which was perceived to be fairer. I was subject to the first lottery drawing and came up with number 302 out of a possible 365. I would not be drafted and would not serve, unless I decided to enlist or apply to Officer Candidate School upon graduation. By this time I had made a firm decision that I wanted to join the NYPD, not the military.

Our nation's poorest and disadvantaged young men would carry a large and disproportionate burden during the Vietnam War. If you could afford to go to college, you had a decent chance of not being called by the draft board. There is something inherently unfair about this, and I witnessed this inequity as my friends who didn't attend college were shipped out to Vietnam after boot camp.

Charlie Patrizio was a classmate of mine at Our Lady of Perpetual Help (OLPH) grammar school. I ate lunch with him just about every day at a small luncheonette called Prisco's. Both Charlie and I lived too far from the school to make it home and back in time for the afternoon bell, so we went to the same luncheonette and ate the same thing every single day—a huge tuna salad hero sandwich and a chocolate egg cream. Neither of us was slim at the time. Charlie's nickname was Choo-Choo because he was such a slow runner, but he had the slickest Elvis Presley hairstyle that you could find. Charlie was a great guy and a good friend, and it still seems inconceivable to me that this 18-year-old kid would have his life ended by stepping on a land mine in

Vietnam. What an absolute waste! During a trip to Washington, D.C., I visited the Vietnam Memorial and touched Charlie's name on the Wall and wept for my grade school classmate.

Vietnam Vets deserve our eternal gratitude because they were faithful sons and daughters of a nation whose government at times seemed to lose its moral compass in the fog of this war. I have the deepest respect for the brothers and sisters of my generation who served during that soul-searching period in America's history. And I shall never forget my lunch pal, Charlie Patrizio.

During 1968 there were a number of sit-ins and disturbances at Columbia University centering on the Vietnam War. The sons and daughters of America's privileged saw fit to protest their opposition to the war in a number of unseemly and ungallant ways, including throwing bricks and bottles at police officers who were sent to this Ivy League university to restore order. My boss at the time was Sergeant Bernie Wease, a bright and easy-going former coal miner from Pennsylvania who was a doctoral candidate and looked the part with his pipe. Bernie had a professorial demeanor and yet he was a tough, barrel-chested cop who never seemed to get rattled.

One spring day some students and professional pro-vocateurs at Columbia decided it was time to riot, so the department mobilized the Police Academy and sent the rookies up to the university along with hundreds of other experienced officers from across the city. Bernie Wease was assigned as a supervisor when the proverbial shit hit the fan and the so-called civilized students did uncivilized things. During the fiasco, Bernie was knocked to the ground and a riotous student jumped on his chest, which resulted in Bernie having a severe heart attack. Another officer was hit in the arm with a brick, which caused a blood clot that ultimately resulted in his death. Now remember, these were America's brightest students who were just trying to show their disdain for our "violent" and "lawless" actions in Vietnam, so "logically" they used violence against others. These Ivy League felons selectively decided what was right and wrong, and found no culpability in their collective acts of wanton violence.

Bernie Wease obviously was incapacitated and ultimately he retired on a disability pension. I was named *Trainee-in-Charge* of the Personnel Testing Unit because I knew the entire operation and the Captain liked the way I took over and tried to keep the ship afloat right after the assault on Bernie. Now there really was no such title in the NYPD, so they made a big deal out of my ceremonial "promotion" at the Police Academy. Although I didn't get a dime more in my paycheck (I was then making $77 per week), I jumped at the opportunity to be in charge of something. Three limited-duty cops who were medically disabled and 3 civilian women, none of whom really got along with each other, staffed the unit. Frankly, nobody else would do this job, so while I considered it a great honor, I'm sure some people thought I was nuts for jumping into this hornet's nest. Well, I made it work and the Captain one day called me aside and said that he was grateful and would help me get the precinct of my choice when I graduated from Recruit Training. I never called on him for the favor because there was only one command I wanted and that was the Tactical Patrol Force, the NYPD's civil disorder and elite anti-crime unit. And I felt I could get into TPF on my own. But first I had to prove myself as *Trainee-in-Charge* and then get through the Police Academy's Recruit Training School.

Chapter 4
Police Academy

D uring 1968 Senator Robert F. Kennedy and the Reverend Martin Luther King, Jr. were assassinated. It seemed that the world was coming apart at the seams, that hope was being driven from America and abject violence took up the first 20 minutes of the half-hour evening news. Each night more caskets would be returned from Vietnam and our nation's most precious resource—its young people— would be laid to rest with full military honors. Flag manufacturers were doing a booming business either supplying the Stars and Stripes for coffins, or selling Old Glory to lowlifes who had the temerity to burn our sacred symbol and offend those who served so gallantly to defend our freedom. America was a divided nation and the police, to some, were the domestic symbols of governmental oppression. This was the venomous message spewing from the mouths of the professional provocateurs who tried to instigate civil disorder on the streets of America.

If you were breathing and lucid during this period, then this irrational behavior and mindless violence had to affect you in some manner. But life went on.

In October I was assigned to Trainee Company 68-S for Recruit Training. I went from being in charge of people to being the lowest of the grunts—a recruit in the Police Academy.

The Police Academy was the institution that transformed you from a civilian to a sworn member of the force. Never again would you be considered part of the civilian world, for the world was divided into two parts—"us and them." Although Sir Robert Peel, the

Founder of London's Metropolitan Police in 1829, said, "The police are the people, and the people are the police," this pithy expression remains an unfulfilled objective rather than a statement of fact. There existed a great divide between America's police departments and the communities they served. This rift was now widened by the radical anti-war crowd; some of its followers embraced the empty promises of communism as opposed to the freedoms America sought to expand and define for all its people through progressive civil rights legislation and enlightened court decisions. To the anti-war radicals, America's military incursions into Southeast Asia established sufficient proof that our nation had lost its soul and could not redeem itself.

Legitimate opposition to the war got lumped in with the harsh rhetoric of the day and sincere Americans with reservations about the war sometimes were unjustly categorized as communist sympathizers. The country roiled with passions from one end of the political continuum to the next as I reported in my gray trainee uniform for Day One at the Police Academy.

Our Company Commander was Sergeant Bobby Corrigan, a veteran cop who had been shot in the line of duty and now served as an Academy instructor. Sergeant Corrigan was one of the good guys; he was approachable and did his best to help us through the academic part of the training, which was not exactly braced by academic rigor. If you stayed awake in class and reviewed your notes and attended the test review sessions—where they essentially gave away the answers to the multiple choice type exams—you could whistle your way through this element of the Police Academy. I actually enjoyed the classroom instruction and still found time to take 12 credits at John Jay, which was conveniently located in the same building as the Academy. I cannot remember anyone flunking out of the Academy during my stay there.

The Physical Training School and the Firearms and Tactics School, however, tested one's mettle. In the gym, you met up with the prototypical drill instructors who sought to make life miserable for all recruits by harassing and screaming at them. Actually, most of the instructors were effective and helpful. However, there were a few blowhards who regaled us with war stories that were apocryphal and invariably painted the story-teller as a hero cop whose superior physical skills saved his life and his partner's. These tales usually work in a class full of rookies, but remember this was a Trainee class and most of the 20-year-olds in this group had been in the department since they were 17, so they could already discern the bullshit from the real McCoy. Some were already cynical and overconfident or "chesty"—as they would say—particularly those who had spent almost four years working in clerical positions at busy precincts.

For me, firearms training was a nightmare. I had never fired a weapon in my life—and it showed. Part of the technique for firing a .38 is not to anticipate the report or noise, which makes you jerk the gun and obviously miss the target. For the first two days of this five-day course I had problems handling the weapon and evidently I got under the skin of the instructor who thought little of embarrassing me in front of my class-mates. But the instructor, to his credit, got me to under-stand the techniques of firing the service revolver and by the end of the course I was shooting in the expert range, which shocked the hell out of me—and the instructor as well. Evidently, the instructor knew how to get the best out of me and his shock techniques worked. After all, this was a life and death proposition, so you wanted to have confidence that you could handle the weapon if you had to use deadly physical force against another human being who, perhaps for no other reason than you were a cop, wanted to take your life.

I had great respect for the weapon even though I was not one to go to the range on my own time and practice. Actually, I found nothing exciting or enjoyable about firing a gun at a paper silhouette.

The gun forced me to buy clothes with the weapon in mind. No longer could I just leave the house with my shirt tucked in and my wallet in my back pocket. Now I had to carry the 4-inch barrel revolver 24 hours a day; department policy required us to do so and to always be ready to intervene in police matters whether we were on duty or not. I liked that responsibility, but now I had to adjust to wearing clothes that helped conceal this gun.

After graduation from the Academy, I purchased a snub-nosed Colt .38 Detective Special with a 2-inch barrel, which was easier to conceal but still quite heavy around the waist. At that time, the ankle holster had not appeared on the scene, so we were left with the choice of the traditional waist holster or shoulder holster when we were off duty or in plainclothes.

The 3-month Academy training program flew by and then it was graduation day, the first time we would don our dress blue uniforms in public. My parents and my grandmother attended the exercises at the 69th Street Armory in Manhattan, where the Mayor of the City of New York, John Lindsay, and Police Commissioner Howard Leary and members of his high command would preside over the ceremonies. I still remember the thrill of it all; I was never so happy in my life.

I truly felt that policing was a calling to do something meaningful in life—and to have fun doing it. I couldn't care less about the salary. I lived at home and, except for my car, had no real expenses to be concerned about at that time. We celebrated at a local Italian restaurant and I could see how proud my parents were of their son, the police officer. I know they were terrified when I originally told them that I wanted to be a cop, but over time I think they applauded this choice, yet I know that they worried every single day when I served in the NYPD. All parents of cops do.

I was ready to hit the streets as a member of the famed Tactical Patrol Force. Now the adventure would begin.

Chapter 5
Tactical Patrol Force

T he Tactical Patrol Force was established in 1959 when the police department recognized the need for a mobile civil disorder unit that could also be deployed in high-crime areas when not on riot duty. To me, TPF was the Marine Corps I had not served in; it was New York City's elite brigade and it was the first unit in, when the proverbial shit hit the fan.

I had no desire to do regular precinct work, even though I knew that is where the rubber meets the road and where policing gets done around-the-clock. I just wanted something different, a unit where you didn't have to fill out a lot of forms, such as accident reports, and where every night you had a good shot at making a collar. There would be no rotating tours of duty, for TPF worked from 6:00 P.M. to 2:00 A.M., with four days on and two days off. That was an added bonus. I could finish college by attending morning classes after a few hours of shuteye.

I also had a concern that precinct work would put me into contact with some of the types of corruption that I had heard about, and even witnessed, when I was a kid hanging around my dad's bar & grill, *The Paradise*. I wanted to believe that things had changed, and I was impressed with TPF's sterling reputation for honesty.

I applied for TPF when I was in the Academy and quickly got a call that I would be interviewed at the 4th Precinct by TPF's Commanding Officer, Deputy Chief Inspector Charles McCarthy, who was widely respected throughout the department. I reported early for my interview and was met by a slim, redheaded lieutenant named John Moore who made me feel welcome and comfortable. I must have looked somewhat nervous, so Lieutenant Moore went out of his way to put me at ease and whispered to me that the Chief was a real gentleman who was looking for candidates just like me. He winked and then escorted me into a dimly lit, fairly small office where Chief McCarthy greeted me, shook my hand and asked me to take a seat as he flipped through my application. The interview took no longer than 10 minutes and the Chief did most of the talking. As he dismissed me, he said, "Welcome aboard," and both of us broke into broad grins. I immediately went to the police equipment bureau where I purchased two sets of TPF collar brass for my uniform. I drove home and held the brass in my hand, constantly glancing at them and smiling like a damn fool all the way back to Bay Ridge.

I really had no idea what TPF did on a daily basis except that it was New York's famous—infamous to some—riot squad. But I didn't care, for I would learn the ropes and be well on my way to becoming a detective, which was my short-term goal. TPF would enable me to make scores of arrests and would be my ticket to the Detective Bureau.

Chapter 6
St. Patrick's Day

A s Murphy's Law would have it, someone in the TPF Office forgot to advise me what squad I was assigned to and when I was to report for duty. On St. Patrick's Day of 1969, I called my new command and spoke to an unhelpful clerical cop who put me on the phone with Lieutenant Moore, who told me that I should report to the 17th Precinct in Manhattan by 1000 hours. It was almost 9:00 A.M. and I told the lieutenant that no one had called me and that it was my understanding that my first tour of duty would be 6:00 P.M. that evening. The lieutenant—ever the consummate gentleman—told me that he was sorry about the mix-up and that my squad had been detailed to the St. Patrick's Day Parade for a 1000x1800 day tour. Moore told me to get there as quickly as possible and he assured me that he would call the 17th and advise my sergeant what had happened.

I showered, put on my uniform and figured I would take the subway to the 17th Precinct, which was located on the eastside of Manhattan—not far from the parade route on New York's famous Fifth Avenue. I started running when I left my apartment building and then quickly figured out that that was a dumb idea. A uniformed cop running down the block signaled trouble and attracted attention, so I slowed and walked briskly to the subway entrance, which was right around the corner from where I lived. I waved to the token clerk and he waved me through the gate because police officers were not required to pay the fare, whether they were in uniform or in civilian clothes. This was a contractual benefit and in return for free rides we were to act as police officers in the event something happened during our ride. Frankly, it felt funny entering the subway without paying, yet I felt special and even somewhat powerful.

More of Murphy's Law—the damn subway was running late as scores of impatient partygoers awaited their ride to the big parade. A few teenage girls teased me about being so young; one in particular flirted unabashedly and pointed out that my face was blushing.

Finally, the train roared into the station. I stepped in and everyone seemed to step aside and let me pass. I thought that was quite respectful, but then it dawned on me that they probably thought that I was a Transit cop because of the TPF on my collar. Some people mistakenly took those initials to mean Transit Police Force, when Transit cops actually wore just TP on their collars.

The ride was uneventful except for a few kids who carried booze to the parade and quickly tried to conceal their contraband as I passed. I glared at the teenagers to let them know I knew the score, but I didn't hassle them. I just wanted to get to the 17th Precinct before the parade stepped off because I knew it would be difficult trying to hook up with a squad in which I knew absolutely no one. Besides, what the hell was I to do with the booze if I confiscated it?

The subway train at last arrived and I then walked as briskly as I could over to the East 51st Street station house. The City was alive and you could sense the energy as people dressed in all sorts of green apparel moved in waves through the streets on their way to the parade.

I entered the precinct and approached the desk officer—a middle-aged lieutenant with a piss-poor attitude—and asked where TPF was located. He just pointed to the back room and never raised his eyes from the police blotter, which is the official logbook for the command. I would quickly find out that many desk officers were arrogant and moody bastards and they particularly liked to embarrass rookies and loved to harass TPFers.

I turned and strolled to the room where I saw a number of uniformed guys with TPF brass on their collars. Al least I made it in time, I thought, as I wiped some sweat from my brow.

I asked one of the cops where I could find Sergeant Harry Smith and he pointed to a tall, well-built guy standing with two other cops. I strolled over and introduced myself to Smith, who had no idea who I was or that he was being assigned another rookie from the Academy. Smith just kept shaking his head. So far the entire day had been an unmitigated disaster—and it was just a little after 10:00 A.M. I could see that I was starting off on the wrong foot with my squad sergeant.

I kind of ambled away from Smith and then saw an Academy classmate who shook my hand and said that he was glad to see me. We had been in the same company at the Academy, although I never hung out with this fellow or really got to know him. In fact, this guy usually stayed to himself. But it was a familiar face and I was grateful for that. Buddy—I'll call him that—told me he had been notified to report to the 17th Precinct last night about 10 o'clock.

About 11:00 A.M. Sergeant Smith conducted roll call at which we were given our parade posts. We were given special instructions that if anything broke out between demonstrators we were to make arrests and get the suspects out of the parade route and into a side street, where we would then put them in paddy wagons or radio cars and transport them to the 17th Precinct. The department had some intelligence information that the hardcore supporters of the Irish Republic who sought a unified Ireland and those who vigorously opposed this position and supported England would duke it out during the parade.

Five minutes after I took my post, fisticuffs broke out not ten feet from me. A wall of blue uniforms moved toward the dozen or so combatants and peace was instantly restored as the lads were whisked away to the precinct. Five minutes on the street and I had already assisted in an arrest. TPF was just where I wanted to be—right in the middle of the action; already I knew I had made a good career choice.

The rest of the parade was uneventful, except for a pretty, young brunette who claimed she won a bet by approaching me and kissing me as her friends looked on and laughed hysterically. I had a feeling a cop was behind the whole stunt, but no one owned up to it. By and large, it turned out to be a great St. Patrick's Day and I felt part of a long and wonderful tradition in New York City.

Chapter 7
Clueless

I left my home at 4:00 P.M. to get to the 71ˢᵗ Precinct, which I figured was no more than a half-hour away from my house. My tour would start at 6:00 P.M., but I had no idea where the hell the precinct was and I wasn't taking any chances with Sergeant Smith, after my inauspicious debut at the 17ᵗʰ Precinct.

I pulled up to the station house on Empire Boulevard in the Crown Heights section of Brooklyn and parked my '65 red Chevy Corvair across the street from the precinct. I placed my PBA card on the dashboard, put on my police cap and then walked a few blocks to find a place for a cup of coffee. I needed to kill some time, so I took a seat at the counter of the luncheonette and ordered apple pie à la mode with vanilla ice cream and a cup of coffee. I sensed that the three guys in this place were displeased by my presence; they acted jumpy. This had to be a bookie joint, so I downed the coffee, left most of the pie, paid the bill, left a tip and got the hell out of there. All I needed now was for Sergeant Smith to see me coming out of what I surmised to be some kind of KG joint, where known gamblers hung out and cops were prohibited from entering. Day 2 had not actually begun and already I had screwed up. I left and headed straight to the precinct; I didn't care how early I was at this point.

As I walked into the 71ˢᵗ Precinct, I saw this cop named Tom, a member of my squad. Tom also was super early so I began to feel more comfortable. I had no idea where to go, so I followed Tom like a puppy trails his mother. We went to the sitting room where, in a little over an hour, roll call would be held. Tom showed me how to record stolen vehicle reports in my memo book, which—under departmental rules and procedures—we were required to do before hitting the streets. Tom was a real gentleman and we got to spend some time together before roll call because we were always the first to arrive at the precinct.

I was nervous before roll call but it was nothing like the level of anxiety I experienced when a half-crazed TPF lieutenant decided to address the outgoing platoon. This lunatic with a crew cut and a squeaky voice jumped on top of a table and started screaming at us at the top of his lungs; his face getting more flushed as he blew off steam. To this day, I have no idea what he said and I left the station house not knowing whether this was a regular part of a TPF roll call.

I couldn't wait to get the hell out of the station house and to my post, even though I had absolutely no idea where it was and how to get to it. The only thing I did know was that Buddy was my partner for the night. We picked up our assigned radio and headed out the door to the precinct. Buddy and I, two green rookies with one day's experience on the job—and that at the St. Patrick's Day Parade—managed to find our post on Ralph Avenue, which was a bad-ass street on the border of both the 75th and 73rd Precincts—two of New York's highest crime areas. All the other cops went for coffee right after roll call; Buddy and I went right to our posts, not out of any sense of duty but because we couldn't find the damn coffee shop the other cops frequented.

A classic case of the blind leading the blind was in the works. Neither of us knew what to do, except walk up and down the street, looking as official as two 21-year-old rookies could. We put on our "game faces" to conceal our basic insecurities, which were not based on physical fear but on not knowing what the hell we were doing. Somehow the Academy had not prepared us for this, and I started to wonder whether it was true what some cynical veterans would say: "Forget about what they taught you at the Academy. The street is different; it has its own rules." Not only that, but TPF had its own rules and nobody told us what the hell they were.

How many times can you walk up and down a short foot post, so we decided to stop cars—lots of cars; in fact, anything that moved got pulled over for a safety check. In a few hours we must have stopped 50 cars and checked licenses and registrations and inspections. We took turns checking out the motorists' credentials as the other guy would pan his flashlight into the car searching for guns and other contraband.

I gave out my first summons for an expired inspection sticker and was pleased that the motorist didn't act up and cause a scene. So far, so good.

The sergeant came by for the first "scratch" of the night, which essentially means that the supervisor can attest that you were on post and alive and well. In TPF, the sergeant—who is the patrol supervisor—signs your memo book around 7:30 P.M. and then you are on your own until around 12:30 A.M., when he returns for the second and final "scratch" or "see" of the tour. Of course, if you need the sergeant for some reason, you can reach him by radio and he'll respond to your post.

The sergeant pulled up and saw that Buddy and I had lined up about six cars at a traffic light and were proceeding to stop all of these motorists, a few of whom were honking their horns. This was not Harry Smith, who I think was covering the other end of the precinct. This middle-aged boss had this puzzled look on his face that said something was amiss.

"Boys, I guess you're catching tonight. Well, be safe and I'll see you later," the sergeant said, as he signed our memo books.

Could it be that this guy had no idea that we were two rookies working together our first night in uniform? Didn't our youthful faces and blank stares belie any assumption that we were experienced cops? Yes, he was right; we were looking to make an arrest. But didn't he know that it would be our first arrest ever? I guess it didn't matter, for he motioned his chauffeur to drive off as he rolled up his window.

After numerous car stops and a few summonses, but no arrests, Buddy and I decided to grab a bite to eat. We jumped into Buddy's car, which he had parked on our post, and headed off to a kosher deli on Eastern Parkway; we then proceeded to annoy the waiter by asking for food, which unbeknownst to us, did not conform to Jewish dietary laws. Multicultural sensitivity training had yet to be introduced to the NYPD.

After the meal, we returned to our post where we stopped a few more cars, gave out some summonses and then waited in a tenement hallway until the sergeant returned for the second scratch. He collected our summonses, shot us that same puzzled look and pulled off into the night. We had no idea why the sergeant had that perplexed look on his face. Maybe that's just the way the guy looked when he saw a couple of cops who had absolutely no idea what the hell they were doing.

About 1:40 A.M. we headed back to the precinct for return roll call. I had worked my first night in the street and, except for some initial anxiety, I enjoyed it and looked forward to tomorrow's tour of duty at the 9th Precinct in Manhattan's famed East Village.

Chapter 8
Alphabet City

T he 9th Precinct had it all—crime, the entertainment of the East Village and its Hippies, and enough places where you could get a decent meal if you wanted to take some time out from the excitement to eat. If you wanted hardcore crime, all you had to do was get a foot post down in Alphabet City—Avenues A, B and C—where narcotics flowed continuously out of run-down tenements, where drug dealers were protected by thugs with guns, and by large, vicious dogs with unsightly mange.

The foot posts on St. Mark's Place provided ample opportunities to observe the free love, drug-obsessed generation that lived under the universal banner of the peace symbol. The tuned-out generation strolled the streets of the East Village, where they would buy their psychedelic drugs and retreat from reality.

There were also visitors who walked the streets out of curiosity, and liked to shop and spend some serious dough in the faddish shops that dotted the neighborhood. And there were the so-called weekend Hippies who made their way down to the East Village, frequently to catch a concert in the famous Filmore East, after wearing conservative business suits and feasting off the free enterprise system all week long. This was the Mecca of the counterculture, and an exciting laboratory to learn about some of America's deep-rooted social problems, and our ineffective responses to them.

The roll call listed the assigned posts and my new partner's name was Risch. I had no idea who the hell this guy was, but at least two rookies would not be paired off again. Someone had noticed this mistake and corrected it, I figured.

I asked Tom—my fellow early bird—to point out Risch and he had no idea whatsoever who the guy was. Not a good sign. Perhaps he was from the other squad since there were two TPF squads working the 9th tonight.

I saw another cop pointing toward me and then this huge cop with a black mustache and long sideburns approached me. A large, outstretched hand preceded this hulking cop who announced that he was Ron Risch. Right away I knew he was another rookie from his shield number, which was 28578—a high number that signified he recently graduated from the Academy. But I knew this guy from somewhere other than the Academy. Then it clicked. We had attended the same high school— Xaverian, in Brooklyn—and now we were partnered together for a tour of duty in the 9th Precinct.

So the police department in its infinite wisdom once again paired two clueless rookies in a high-crime precinct. The whole thing bordered on bureaucratic insanity, yet this was nothing short of standard operating procedure in the NYPD at the time. But what rookie would dare question that wacky lieutenant who screamed gibberish and seemed full of rage?

So, Ronnie Risch and I went with the flow; we took our posts and followed the rest of the guys to the nearest coffee shop, where every tour of duty in TPF began. The late Dr. Arthur Niederhoffer, a former NYPD police lieutenant, wrote in his seminal work on policing, *Behind the Shield*, that police officers drink coffee in the beginning of their tour, as a kind of libation to the gods, to protect them from the evil forces that they may encounter while on patrol. Traditions die hard in the NYPD, so even today, thousands of cups of coffee will be consumed by

New York's Finest. Don your protective vest, hit the streets, and down a cup of Java.

Risch and I got assigned to a post on Avenue C and right away we assisted another TPF team in making a heroin collar. There was an art to making a collar in Alphabet City. Actually, the collars were there for the asking; the real trick was transporting your prisoner away from the scene to the precinct before the garbage started coming off the rooftops at you. Bad guys made a sport out of it. Skells loaded up with milk bottles, garbage and even trash cans and waited for the opportunity to skull some cop making a collar, or in some instances just walking his beat. Incidentally, skell is a New York term for criminals and those who have a propensity for acts of social deviance. There were a lot of skells in the 9th Precinct. It was a great place to work!

One night I turned a corner and walked into 7th Street, from Avenue C, when a guy around 18 years old looked me square in the eye and turned on his heels and ran like hell. I absolutely knew this guy was dirty, but I also knew that in a foot race this guy would win the gold medal. I started to run after him and I noticed a bulge under his shirt, which was not tucked into his pants. So I flung my nightstick at him and incredibly the nightstick caught him in the back of his knee and the fleeing sprinter crashed to the ground. I mean this was a work of art. I jumped on his back and instantly a garbage can landed three feet to my right. The prisoner resisted as I struggled to cuff him. My partner commandeered a gypsy cab and we rushed my prized prisoner back to the precinct. He had ten decks of heroin on him; he had just copped his drugs moments before our eyes made contact. The bulge turned out to be nothing more than one of those biker wallets connected to a chain that he clipped onto his belt. But I didn't know that at the time and I felt I had to stop him because the guy was definitely up to no good. How did I know that this guy hadn't just committed a violent crime? As far as the search being admissible, well, I wrote up the affidavit exactly the way the incident happened, and the kid took a plea. His Legal Aid attorney probably figured a "no jail time" plea served everyone's purpose, and so that's the tack they took.

That was the first and last time I threw a nightstick, which was essentially a spontaneous reaction on my part. In retrospect, I recognized that the entire incident was dicey and pushed the envelope. But being young inspires a belief in your absolute invincibility and complete confidence in your decisions.

Professor Niederhoffer may have been on to something, for the gods were certainly looking out for me that night in the 9th Precinct. I know one thing, I was damned lucky the trash can missed its target.

To this day, I still drink a lot of coffee!

Chapter 9
Partners

T here is this almost ritualistic courting period that precedes the formal pairing of partners; it centers on discovering if the person you're working with essentially shares your values. On a more practical level is the question as to whether you can stand to be with this person for eight hours a day.

It doesn't take long for the partners to figure out if theirs is a bad marriage. When a cop knows that the marriage has been made in hell, he or she will discreetly talk to the sergeant "in code"—so to speak— and request another match-up. Unless the relationship is on the border of dissolving into a gun battle, then the protocol dictates that you not badmouth the other guy to the sergeant. You more or less talk around the issue and the sergeant usually pairs you off with someone else.

Ronnie Risch and I hit it off immediately and the deal was sealed. We became partners and to this day remain close friends. Our first night together on patrol was basically uneventful, after we assisted another team make a heroin collar. But we spent a lot of time talking and feeling each other out—and we clicked. By being partnered we also avoided the close scrutiny and hazing that other rookies got when paired off with veterans who were disgruntled that they were teamed with kids right out of the Academy. Risch and I formed a comfort zone and—since both of us considered ourselves street-wise—we figured we'd keep our eyes and ears open and learn the job on our own.

Before Ronnie and I hooked up, I once had to visit Harry Smith before roll call, to indicate in vague terms that I could not work with this other rookie. Harry just nodded and I got the impression that he had already heard this from someone else. A few years later the guy I didn't want to work with would be arrested and incarcerated for shooting someone in an off-duty incident. This was the same officer I worked with my first night on the street in the 71st Precinct. I actually liked Buddy, but I thought he made poor decisions at times and that he often lacked the discretion needed to be an effective police officer.

I have come to understand that you should always trust your gut; it can save your life in the police business and in life in general. Your instincts are your best friends; don't ignore them.

Trust your gut, pick your partners carefully and, in most instances, things will work out. And, of course, it never hurts to be lucky!

Chapter 10
The Great White Way

I t was time to make my Broadway Debut, so we reported to the 18th Precinct in midtown Manhattan. Ronnie and I got assigned to 42nd Street along with about ten other TPF cops. We literally saturated the block with cops and we still didn't put much of a dent in crime on The Great White Way.

On this famous boulevard you could buy just about anything illegal that you wanted, from drugs to weapons to women. The department deployed so many cops on this block because, within minutes of being assigned there, one of us would make a collar and then it was off to the races. The art of making an arrest on 42nd Street was to strike quickly and hustle your prisoner off to the station house, before the crowd would interfere and try to take your prisoner away from you. Yes, that's right. Skells would get foolish and attempt to interfere with the arrest and then they also would be hauled off to the 18th Precinct.

One night TPF was called into a porn movie house, where one of New York's upstanding citizens was engaged in an act of self-gratification, to put it mildly, that offended another member of the audience, if you can believe that anyone in such a decrepit place could be offended by anything. Anyway, the manager walked outside and asked a couple of TPF cops to witness this unseemly but fairly common event. The cops grabbed the skell and whisked him out of the movie, as many in the audience booed the cops and then followed them outside. Once outside, these perverts and some other creeps hanging around 42nd Street, just looking for trouble, began to harass the cops. I saw what was happening and ran over to help out. For some reason, there was a delay in getting a radio car to transport the prisoner, so the arresting officers commandeered a taxicab and ordered the driver to take them to the station house. To my absolute amazement, the cabby flatly refused to transport them, which by law he must do. Without missing a beat, another TPF cop opened the taxi door, grabbed the driver, cuffed him and threw him in the back seat, right next to the guy with the weird smile and the open fly. The crowd now got into it and tried to overturn the taxi. Only on 42nd Street! We had to call for some reinforcements to reestablish order.

As usual, order was quickly restored and then, within minutes of the movie caper, I grabbed a guy carrying a sword cane and locked him up for possession of a dangerous instrument. There was this new fad amongst the street people, involving what appeared to be a harmless walking cane, but inside of it, when you pulled out the handle, was a long and sharp sword. I got quite adept at distinguishing real canes from the swords and started to compile some felony collars, which were easy arrests to make and prosecute. After a while, you would think that even these witless felons would realize that to walk down 42nd Street with a sword cane was tantamount to wearing a neon light that flashed, "Lock me up!" Yet just about every night some nitwit would stroll into a waiting pair of handcuffs held by a smiling TPF cop, who then whisked the fool off to the zoo called night court.

═══════════════════════════

One night our unit got mobilized to the scene of a potential civil disorder in Brooklyn where, after patrolling the streets for a couple of hours, the bosses decided that we would be better deployed in Manhattan at the 18th precinct. On the trip to midtown Manhattan one of the guys fell asleep on the TPF bus and this triggered a reaction from the restless gallery of pranksters. First, they took the guy's shield off his jacket and pinned it back upside down. Then someone got the idea that it would be funny to remove his weapon from its holster, which would cause the guy to panic and think that he had lost his gun in Brooklyn. In its place someone inserted a banana. Everyone laughed hysterically as the bus traveled to the 18th Precinct.

Incredibly, no one put the gun back when we arrived in Manhattan. So for some 10 minutes this cop walked his post with his police shield upside down and a banana in his holster. Thank God it was winter, and the long coat that we wore during those days, concealed the holster. What if the cop had to pull his weapon and out comes a banana? After that episode no one ever again removed any guns from holsters. The victim of this stunt went ballistic, and nobody ever needled him about his Colt .45 banana. Police humor can be fiercely funny, but this one was admittedly beyond the pale.

On another mobilization to Coney Island one terribly humid day in August, our police bus was traveling through the Battery Tunnel from Manhattan to Brooklyn, when the driver in front of us ignored our turret lights and siren, and refused to move over into the other lane and let the bus pass. The bus driver, who was an easygoing guy, pounded on the siren and just couldn't fathom why this idiot in front of us would block us from responding to a police emergency. As we exited the tunnel, a TPFer from another squad opened the window of the bus and mooned the driver of the obstructionistic car. Others hooted and called the driver a few choice words, and shot him the bird, as motorists lining up to pay their tolls had to be shocked and scandalized by this police behavior. Furthermore, they had absolutely no idea what precipitated it. The sergeant in the lead car of the caravan also had no idea what was taking place behind him, that one of his men had his bare ass hanging out of a police bus, with scores of witnesses taking in the whole show.

In many ways, some cops lived on the edge and their actions sometimes reflected their over-the-top attempt at humor. But from a community relations and at times public safety perspective, these actions were puerile, unacceptable and downright dumb!

Believe it or not, nothing ever resulted from the bus incident. Even if a civilian reported the event, one would have to pause and question the description of this episode. I mean, you're telling me that in broad daylight a New York City cop had his bare ass protruding from a marked police bus that had its lights on and siren blasting, as his colleagues in blue were spewing forth epithets and giving the middle finger to the traumatized driver of a Chevy? Yeah, right!

I just can't imagine that such an incident would happen today or, if it did, that it would go unreported. In fact, there's a good chance that the entire affair would be videotaped and sold to the highest bidder.

The 18th Precinct offered a different slice of New York City. You had Broadway shows, newly released flicks, wide-eyed tourists and servicemen walking up and down the Great White Way and, of course, the endless parade of prostitutes and street skells. Lowlife pimps, promising teenagers the world in return for their servitude, would approach young runaways exiting the Port Authority Bus Terminal. Frightened kids, from all parts of America and beyond, would flee their homes for the so-called freedom and adventure of New York City and then be trapped into a life of drugs and prostitution. Despicable pimps would ply them with drugs and beat the hell out of them until these poor kids would comply with their pimps' demands.

Cops despise pimps; they fall on the food chain just slightly above rapists and child molesters. During the 1960s and 1970s, pimps would flaunt their disdain for the law and the police by driving through midtown Manhattan in what was commonly labeled pimpmobiles. These gaudy and custom-modified Cadillac convertibles would be driven by some punk all made up in his best pimp suit, which usually was topped off by a white fur coat and wide-brimmed hat. The entire getup said, "Screw you. You're out there walking a beat like a jerk and I'm driving around in my Caddy, just waiting to collect my dough from my girls." Pimps were bold assholes and they expected to get stopped at every corner—and TPF obliged them every single night.

Of course, all of these pimpmobiles were properly registered, inspected and had insurance, so there was no expectation that TPF would find something wrong with these cars. But they would still be thoroughly inspected by TPF. One night, however, a TPF team stopped a pimpmobile and the cops hit pay dirt. The dumb pimp forgot to bring along his license and registration, so it was off to the 18th Precinct for a "thorough" auto investigation, as it was called during those days. The pimp was embarrassed and starting to jaw at the cops, which is not a good idea, because the whole thing could escalate and the pimp would then find himself locked up for disorderly conduct, resisting arrest, obstructing governmental administration and any other violation that the cops could find in the New York State Penal Law and the Vehicle and Traffic Law, or any other law for that matter. The pimp, and the two prostitutes who were his passengers, were hauled into the precinct as the cops went through a purposely long and laborious process to make certain that the car was legitimate.

The cop who drove the pimpmobile to the station house honked the horn and was cheered by the other

uniformed cops assigned to the various posts on Broadway and on 42nd Street. The whole circus-like event was
a morale booster for the troops who had a visceral
disdain for pimps, and a compassionate concern for the
teenage prostitutes hooked into a life of hell by these
contemptible punks.

As expected, the car was completely legit, and the
pimp left the station house with a few summonses and a
major league attitude, after having been detained and
embarrassed in front of his "girls." The pimpmobile had
been parked down the block from the precinct, in a place
where both the platoon that was getting off duty and the
outgoing platoon would have to pass it on their way to
and from the station house. As the story goes, one
frustrated and deeply angry cop who hated what pimps
did to their victims, took it upon himself to whack the
pimpmobile with his nightstick as he passed. This
precipitated a chain reaction, so to speak, where other
cops also took swings at this visible symbol of what was
wrong with society and the criminal justice system in
particular. By the time Mr. Pimp got to his wheels it
looked like a beer can that had been stomped on by a
bunch of enthusiastic school kids. The headlights were
smashed and the car was full of wrinkles from the
hammering it took from the nightsticks. The story has it
that the pimp just drove off and never made a complaint.
I suppose he didn't want to go back into the station
house to file a complaint; it just wouldn't be good for
business, and I guess he figured that his fellow pimps
would not like the heat that they would get from such an
action. So he drove off and probably bought a brand new,
shiny pimpmobile the next morning. But I'll bet he never
forgot his license and registration again.

Was this behavior understandable? Perhaps. But cops
must not engage in street justice, even in the face of such
deviant and arrogant behavior by these lowlifes. The

whole affair captures the collective frustration that cops feel, and it demonstrates that this pent-up frustration can manifest itself into spontaneous acts of self-gratification that are ethically and legally perilous to the cops involved. There is simply no place for street justice in the criminal justice system, yet there are times when reasonable and decent people agree that such actions seem justifiable and deserving. But they are dead wrong!

I did not take a swipe at the pimpmobile. But I have to admit that at the time I was not filled with righteous indignation about the incident.

The Broadway show called *The 18th Precinct* turned out to be a morality play, a long-playing one. I just didn't understand its meaning and implications at the time. Now I do. Emotions and subjective reasoning must not drive the actions of those whose duty it is to enforce the laws within the constraints of the U.S. Constitution. Beating the hell out of a pimpmobile may be momentarily gratifying, but it demeans both the law and the cops who, lemming-like, follow the thoughtless actions of a fellow officer seeking to work out his frustrations on a material symbol of society's decadence.

Professionalism demands that the police service never pursue extra-legal solutions to pressing, and even sometimes, heart-breaking problems, such as teen prostitution. Such a road is paved with nothing more than expedient and unethical solutions to deep-rooted social problems.

Chapter 11
In Hot Pursuit

M

y TPF unit spent many nights patrolling the high-crime precincts of Brooklyn North, where arrests were plentiful and supervision was almost nonexistent, except for the two scratches from the sergeant at 7:30 P.M. and 12:30 A.M. every tour of duty. There was this unwritten rule in TPF that, as long as you didn't screw up, the bosses would basically let you do your thing on the streets. This generally meant that you could roam off your assigned posts to make collars and you could go to eat with your partner if you wanted. Department procedure dictated that you were to eat at assigned times and that one member of the team should remain on post as the other ate his meal. This rule may have been enforced in certain Manhattan precincts, such as Greenwich Village and Midtown, but in Brooklyn North no one I know ever followed procedure, and these unwritten rules had the tacit approval of the squad sergeant.

One night I hooked up with another rookie, (I'll call him Willie) and we took our foot post in the 83rd Precinct. Ronnie Risch had made a collar the night before and had spent the entire day in court, so he took the night off. Willie was a character: a German-American with blonde hair and blue eyes and bulging biceps, that were developed from his moonlighting job of delivering dairy products during the early hours of the morning. I have no idea when and if Willie ever slept. He said that one of his goals was to drive a truck filled with nitroglycerine; he wanted to live his entire life living on the edge. Willie was a character, all right.

This midsummer evening Willie and I were conducting car stops, when a moron decides to run on us. In
doing so he almost clipped Willie, who had positioned
himself a bit too close to the car for comfort's sake. As
the car left rubber Willie took a swipe with his nightstick
and left a dent on the rear fender. We stopped a passing
motorist and told the elderly driver to try to follow the
Chevy, but to take it easy and not speed. We made a
point to tell the driver that he was not to go through any
traffic lights or blow any stop signs. I radioed our position to the TPF base operator, who was back at the 83rd
Precinct, and asked for assistance as I described the car
and gave its location. The skell who ran on us didn't
seem to have any idea we were behind him and after
about a mile or so, he pulls over to the curb. The old guy
driving us got a kick out of the whole thing and per-
formed like a professional wheelman.

Willie and I make our way out of the car and start
walking toward the guy, when he notices us and reaches
back into the car and comes out with a machete, which
he now holds up to us in a menacing way, as he starts to
walk toward us. We both pull our guns and scream at
him to drop the machete or he's a dead man. The guy
just grins and continues to move toward us, but at a
slower pace. Willie and I make some eye contact and
then we charge the son-of-a-bitch and drive him against
the side of a fence as the machete falls harmlessly to the
sidewalk. As we slammed him into the fence, I could
smell the liquor on his breath and knew right away that
this moron was dead drunk, and he was damn lucky he
wasn't filled with lead.

Willie and I handcuffed the bum as a TPF radio car
pulled up to transport our prisoner to the 83rd Precinct to
be booked.

Later that evening, Willie and I talked about the
entire experience and we both admitted that it shook us

up. It wasn't the danger that we focused on in our conversation; rather, it had to do with the fact that we were close to shooting this guy and had the legal right to do so. But we chose to tackle him because something intuitively told us that this would be the better course of action—and in light of his intoxicated state, it turned out to be just that. This guy was bombed; he couldn't even talk he was so drunk, and he blew something like a .19 on the Breathalyzer. Had we fired our weapons we would be appearing before a grand jury to justify our actions. More important, no one in his right mind wants to shoot another person if there is another alternative available. We diagnosed the situation accurately and no one got hurt. Sure, I would think a grand jury would understand that we thought our lives were in jeopardy and therefore it was reasonable to fire at someone coming at us with a machete. It would have been a legally correct shooting, but it would not have been great police work.

Willie and I handled this situation in a professional manner and took on additional risks. But that's what policing is all about. Another place, another time, under similar circumstances, working with another cop may have produced a different outcome. Who knows?

Policing deals with the uncertainties and unpredictable elements of life under extraordinary stressful conditions. A misdiagnosis that night could have gotten Willie or me an Inspector's Funeral. No one seeks that honor, not even a consummate risk-taker like Willie.

Chapter 12
Police-Community Relations

T he 73rd Precinct covered the Ocean Hill-Brownsville section of Brooklyn, a high-crime area that was plagued by violent crimes and arson. One of the most perplexing things I ever encountered in TPF involved the New York City Fire Department, which deservedly goes by the nickname "New York's Bravest." For some incomprehensible reason, firefighters responding to alarms to save lives and property were bombarded with bottles, bricks, garbage cans and anything else hurled from rooftops by neighborhood punks.

The media gave this story a lot of play and even offered some reasons why this was happening. Some pundits suggested that the community was striking back at government for its failed urban renewal policies; the Fire Department, they reasoned, presented a visible and easy target for all of this pent-up aggression. Other, more practical-minded commentators suggested that these uncourageous thugs picked firemen as their targets because unlike cops the smoke eaters didn't carry guns.

So it was that TPF got assigned to ride shotgun for fire trucks in this troubled area. This simple strategy actually worked. Incidents were reduced and the story moved to the back pages of New York's newspapers.

I vividly remember how hard these firefighters worked every night. They never returned the rig to the firehouse because in a matter of minutes another alarm would come in and off they would race to another fire. These guys were covered with soot and dirt and had to lose five pounds every tour from perspiring.

I said to myself that there was no way in the world that I would want any part of their job. I feared fire and heights; I would have made some firefighter! No way. These firefighters liked to tell us that they wanted no part of policing and always reminded us that firemen never left the FDNY to go to the NYPD; it was always the other way around. I cannot think of one guy who ever left the Fire Department to become a cop. I know of dozens, however, who bolted the NYPD as soon as they got their appointment letter from the Fire Department. I wouldn't even take the civil service test for firefighter. Most people have a specific set of fears and may even be phobic about some things. Just keep me away from ladders and smoke.

Now, having said all this, let me tell you a story about the dog in the abandoned building. One day Ronnie Risch and I are making our way down Saratoga Avenue, which is our assigned foot post for this evening tour in the 73rd Precinct. All of a sudden we hear this squealing and crying and barking from a dog that somehow got his paw caught in a fire escape some three stories up in this burned-out, abandoned tenement. The dog is panicking and so Ronnie and I walk into the building and are welcomed by scores of huge rats that scamper away, but not too far away for comfort's sake. (Incidentally, add rats to my list of fears. I detest them.)

I figure we can make our way up the staircase and get this dog out of his predicament. But there are no stairs, just the remnants of a staircase. Back to the drawing boards. The ladder for the fire escape is down and I can reach it from the street. Against the better judgement of Ronnie, I decide to climb up a few rungs to see if Plan B will work. So far so good, so I start my climb to save the Red Baron.

I reach him and the mutt starts licking me, and his tail starts to wag like an out of control pendulum. I release his paw and now wonder what the hell I'm going to do with this mixed breed, who stays close to my leg and starts licking my uniform pants.

Because it's raining, I have my raincoat with me, which I fashion into something resembling a bag. I figure I'll put the mutt into this makeshift sack and carry him down with my left arm, as I use the right hand to grasp the fire escape.

I pick him up and start my slow descent, praying that this dog doesn't get spooked and bite me because his head is now bobbing around my face. I'm just past the second floor when the damn ladder breaks from one of its two hooks. The pooch and I are now swinging back and forth, from side to side. Risch quickly jumps on top of a garbage can and stabilizes the ladder from below, as I slowly make my way down with the dog licking my face every step of the way. The last hook held and we make it down to the street where Risch is pale and speechless.

I actually thought about taking the dog back to my dad's bar after work, but abandoned that idea and let him walk off into the night. To this day, I have no idea how that dog got there and can't believe that I—the guy who has always feared heights—would do such a stupid stunt. It was impulsive and, while it worked out in the end, I could have been seriously hurt or even killed trying to save the dog. I think part of my reasoning—if by any stretch you could call it that—had to do with the fact that I would have been embarrassed to call the Fire Department, because these guys were so overworked that I felt they didn't need "a save the dog" call from TPF. Not in the 73rd Precinct anyhow.

All Ronnie could do was shake his head. Later he would ask me how a college graduate could do something so dumb. I really couldn't answer that, but I told him he should nominate me for an ASPCA letter of commendation. He said I should get a letter of commitment to Creedmore Psychiatric Hospital. He may have had a point.

I also learned about prejudice and discrimination while patrolling the streets of the 73rd Precinct. One night a group of young kids were playing stickball in the street. As we approached them, the kids started to get a little uneasy and some of them just stared at us to see what we were going to do. I asked the kid with the broom handle bat if I could take a swing and he handed over the bat. The kids were in an age range of say 11 to 14; all of them were black. The pitcher released the ball and I swung and missed. The kids cheered. I got hold of the next pitch and hit it almost two sewers, not a bad shot. I could sense the kids were loosening up a bit. For a few moments, everyone seemed to have some fun. But then a middle-aged man yelled at his kid to come to him; the boy looked embarrassed and darted off to his dad. Another adult also screamed at his kid to leave the game immediately. The game stopped and the kids walked off. I could hear the first guy tell his kid that we were the "enemy," that the kid should have nothing to do with us, ever. The kid started to cry and his father pulled him away by the arm.

I felt terrible for a number of reasons. Some of the kids were in trouble because of me and may get punished by their parents for consorting with the "enemy." That was not right. Nor was it right that someone should label me the enemy and fill those kids' hearts with prejudice because we wore blue uniforms. Weren't we doing what we were supposed to be doing—building bridges to the community by establishing a rapport with the kids of the neighborhood? Sure, I suppose some of those people had legitimate gripes against the cops; maybe some of them had been mistreated in the past. But it was wrong to label all cops as the enemy; that was bigotry and it was equally as despicable as labeling someone an enemy because of his or her race, creed, or ethnicity. This event gave me insight into prejudice and discrimination, and demonstrated in concrete terms, the deep divide that existed between the police and the community.

I don't think we have progressed all that much over the last three decades in strengthening police-community relations. I do believe that it is possible to continue to reduce crime and build strong and lasting relationships with the diverse communities of New York City. Both of these goals are not mutually exclusive and can be attained by creative and bold leadership. Aggressive crime fighting does not have to be incompatible with forging strong bonds with the community.

The major challenge facing the police service involves establishing a working partnership with diverse communities that are changing rapidly throughout our nation. America will continue to be home to immigrants from around the globe, and our justice system must be sensitive to these transformations and adept at serving diverse communities.

But first off, we need to recruit qualified cops; there is now a shortage of police candidates, so this issue must be addressed head-on if we expect to demand professional service from police departments across the nation. This is the first time in my lifetime when police departments are having a difficult time attracting candidates— not just qualified candidates—but people just willing to take the entrance test. This is not totally unexpected, for a strong economy tends to attract young people to occupations and professions where the material rewards far outpace those offered by civil service positions. Interestingly enough, as the private sector's job market contracts—as it has over the last year—then more candidates will be attracted to public service opportunities. Police recruiting is more successful during economic down cycles, but that is only part of the recruitment problem.

Young people now ask themselves, particularly college graduates, why would I want to be a cop? Why should I enter a department when there is no real incentive for college grads in most uniformed agencies? And it seems that the public and the media are always second-guessing the police after a shooting or some other controversial event, even when the cops are right or they made a mistake but acted in good faith. The young people figure, why not go to the federal government? Or maybe law school? And, they ask, why do I need the stress that goes along with being a cop? These are good questions and the police service has not responded with compelling answers to make police work appear more attractive than other opportunities in the criminal justice system. Potential candidates gravitate toward careers where they believe they will be more satisfied, better compensated and will have more balanced and, consequently, happier home lives.

Just four years ago when I polled my class to determine how many students wanted to enter policing, I usually had about a third of the kids' hands go up. Today I get one or two at the most. Sometimes I get no one interested in joining the NYPD. This is regrettable because there is a dire need for good and decent people to become honest and competent police officers who want to serve their communities. But until we address the structural problems in the system that inhibit qualified applicants from seeking careers in blue, we shall continue to muddle through and not all that well. And until we recruit and train people who believe that it is the goal of policing to establish a partnership with the communities they serve, then we will be unable to bridge the divide that creates this expansive gulf between the cops and the people. We will continue the "us versus them" mentality that fuels the distrust and even disdain between the community and its cops.

We can do better—and we must!

Chapter 13
On the Arm

W ashington Square Park in New York's famous Greenwich Village was a hotbed of drug activity during the 1960s and 1970s. Hippies, wannabes, draft dodgers and the usual curious public made their way into this public park that is adjacent to New York University. Street people peddled marijuana and TPF would swarm in and collar these dolts. I liked working the 6th Precinct because there was always some action going on with drug busts and car stops and even with the local cops.

One July evening after turning out of the 6th Precinct, Ronnie and I and about 10 TPF cops headed over to a fast-food joint where we would have our coffee and cake before hitting our posts. It was the type of place where you lined up at the counter to get your order and then paid the cashier at the end of the line. All of us paid and then took a few tables in the back of the restaurant. After sitting for a few minutes, two cops from the 6th Precinct—not TPFers—came in for their coffee and, before you knew it, there were words between the precinct cops and a couple of TPF guys. It seemed that the precinct cops or "hairbags"—as we called veteran cops—took offense to our gathering in this particular restaurant because they felt we were "contract busters," which essentially meant that they were getting their coffee and donuts for free, and felt that we would jeopardize this cozy arrangement because we were all "eating on the arm." Well, we weren't eating for free, and TPF didn't "eat on the arm." TPF was known as a unit that was as clean as a hound's tooth, so it was not our practice to seek out places that let cops eat for free. The whole thing about seeking out free food was just so demeaning—and it was wrong!

The argument started to escalate, but cooler heads prevailed and the cops from the precinct finally left the place with their coffee and buns—but with little or no dignity. We were pissed off, so in typical TPF fashion of taking no prisoners, we went outside and ticketed every double-parked car in sight. This was our message back to the precinct boys. You mess with us; we'll send you a stronger message. Screw your contracts!

There are no free meals in life. In exchange for free coffee, the merchant expects something in return. It's human nature.

Shoppers often double-park and then run into a coffee shop or some other store, such as a dry cleaners. The cops have the discretion to handle the situation in a variety of legal ways. A warning could suffice; a cop does not always have to issue a summons. But in this case, it seemed that there was some kind of *quid pro quo* going on, that permitted illegal parking in exchange for free coffee and food.

Since the precinct cops saw fit to try to embarrass us, they got a verbal barrage from TPF, followed by a ticket blitz. Unfortunately, citizens would pay the price of the parking fines.

We wallpapered the block with summonses and shortly after this a precinct sergeant questioned us about our assigned posts. This was a no-no. Precinct bosses stayed away from us because we had our own supervisors, and frankly, there was never any love lost between precinct personnel and TPF. Many of us in TPF felt that the precinct cops had lost the battle against crime and that is why we were brought in to straighten things out. No one could ever say that we lacked confidence or opinions. But it was not entirely fair to state that the precinct failed because we were now deployed at the crime "hot spots." There were obviously more variables involved here, but it was part of our *esprit de corps* that we were the department's elite crime fighting outfit, so we were not going to do anything to disabuse people of that notion.

This was a tense night in the streets, but it had nothing to do with crime. This battle involved TPF against the arrogance and nonfeasance and malfeasance of these two precinct cops who evidently wanted to make this some kind of an "us against them" battle. How the hell were these assholes going to win? Certainly not on legal or ethical grounds. Was some big boss going to tell us not to issue parking summonses? Now that would make a good media story! And was some police bigwig going to address the issue of the freebies that the precinct guys were getting? I don't think so. Yeah, somebody could make an issue out of the fact that all of us were technically off post and having coffee at the same time in the same place. But that was not the real issue and everyone knew that.

The cold war came to a halt when some TPF bosses met with their counterparts at the precinct level and, although we had to be a little more circumspect in our actions in the 6th Precinct for a while, in a few weeks things returned to normal—if there is such a thing in Greenwich Village. I often wondered what the civilians thought that night in the coffee shop as they witnessed this debacle created by two cops who had little self-respect and found it important to question brother officers about actions for which *they* should have been embarrassed. I guess they felt that "eating on the arm" was something well worth fighting for, so embarrassing themselves in public was a small price to pay for a free cup of coffee. As far as I'm concerned, they were poor excuses for cops.

Chapter 14
Checks and Balances

O ne night Ronnie and I were assigned a foot post around the perimeter of Washington Square Park, the type of post from which you could move in and out of the crowded park and also make some car stops at the various intersections that surrounded the park.

We were in the process of stopping a car full of teenagers, when a woman screamed, "Police, help! He stabbed him. Police!"

Ronnie and I let the car go and ran toward the woman who pointed out a man she said had done the stabbing. Ronnie grabbed the guy who evidently figured that his best chance of avoiding detection was to meld into the crowd and go with the flow and coolly exit the park. Well, this single-minded woman was not about to let that happen and Ronnie collared the creep who, interestingly, didn't resist or try to run off. I rushed toward the victim who had been stabbed with a small knife, that was still imbedded in the elderly man's chest. The victim was conscious, but in a lot of pain, and probably bordering on going into shock because of the blood loss. I called for an ambulance and a radio car to transport the prisoner.

Six TPF cops quickly arrived as Ronnie brought over the alleged perp to see if the victim could identify him, which he did immediately, by calling him a "no-good son-of-a-bitch," among other things. The old guy was feisty and it made me feel that he would survive. Ronnie already had the cuffs on the punk, as a TPF van pulled into the park to transport the prisoner back to the 6th Precinct. Ronnie held the victim's stolen wallet in his hand; the inept robber didn't even have the smarts to drop it before being collared. This guy was dumb as a stump, yet vicious.

Right away I could see that Ronnie was troubled by the incident; he looked distracted and yet I could see that he was full of anger and disgust. Another cop agreed to stay with the victim and escort him in the ambulance, as Ronnie and I put the handcuffed skell in the van. About a block from the park, Ronnie exploded with rage and started to lunge at the prisoner while calling him every epithet under the sun. I grabbed him and held him from going at the punk, who had to think that this was his last day on earth. I had never seen Ronnie blow up like that; it was uncharacteristic and a complete aberration. He was deeply affected by the vicious attack on the poor old man and it just spilled over, and he wanted a piece of the predator.

In this profession, such reactions can be understandable, yet you cannot allow your emotions to get the best of you. This is where self-discipline is needed to protect you from yourself. Actually, what generally happens when such an incident occurs is your partner protects you from doing something you know you will regret and which could conceivably blow the entire case and cost you your job. In this case I had done for Ronnie what he had done for me when a junkie spat in my face as I questioned him. The drug addict then ran off through the streets. We chased him and collared the little punk. In the precinct, the skell mouthed off and spat at me again and now I wanted a piece of the bastard. Ronnie intervened and provided the "checks and balances" that are expected from experienced partners.

Cops see things that are terribly distressful; they see the violent horror that people commit against strangers and even loved ones. Years ago, Dr. William Kroes wrote a book about police stress that was titled *Society's Vic-*

tim—The Police Officer. I think that title aptly depicts the role of the contemporary police officer and what he or she faces over a career of witnessing horrific acts of violence. When people come to understand the horror that police officers witness, they come to understand that cops are also victims—victims of the darkest side of humanity.

A member of the NYPD's Crime Scene Unit tells the story of a precinct detective who at the scene of a horrific murder/suicide had to be restrained from attacking the corpse of a child killer. The cop cognitively knew that the murderer was dead, but his anger and sadness over-whelmed him as he attempted to pummel the dead body, as tears of anguish drained from the detective's eyes. I think even the most ardent police bashers would agree that there was certainly another victim in this tragic case.

Partners need one another to protect themselves from falling prey to the emotions that ordinary men and women feel and often act upon. But in policing, extraor-dinary behavior and self-discipline are required and expected and demanded from the men and women in blue. It is no wonder that there is a national shortage of candidates for the police service. Indeed, police are society's forgotten victims—and we should never forget this. But we cannot use this as a justification for unethical and illegal conduct. Never!

Chapter 15
Civilian Brutality

W e were spending an inordinate amount of time in Crown Heights at the 71st Precinct, where rumor had it that the politically powerful Hasidic community had been influential in making sure their neighborhood was well protected. No one could blame a community for trying to get more police protection, but it became an irritant to many TPF cops because it was now more difficult to make street collars in this precinct, since there were cops all over the place. Besides that, some people felt that the community received preferential treatment to the detriment of other areas of the city that also deserved increased patrol coverage because of their high-crime rates.

One night, Buddy—my Academy classmate—and I got assigned to a foot post at a busy intersection, where we proceeded to make car stops. Car stops could always produce something in the way of drunk drivers and forged licenses, which seemed to be the latest fad.

The traffic light changed to red and I approached a car with only a driver, no passengers. I asked for the driver's license and registration and the motorist said absolutely nothing; he stared straight ahead. I asked again, and the same thing happened. I figured this guy had to be dirty and was waiting for the light to change and then he would bolt, since there were no cars in front of him.

The light changed and the guy does nothing; he just stares blankly ahead. I ask once again, but it's clear that this guy is unresponsive and I'll have to do something. But what?

I am not going to reach in and turn off the guy's ignition because I know that the only cop ever killed in TPF was dragged to his death as he tried to do just that. Now there are about a dozen cars behind this mope and the drivers are getting impatient and hitting their horns. Buddy is watching this guy from the passenger's side because both of us have the feeling this character is about to do something. But he just stares ahead.

I ask him again for his license and registration and this time he explodes and calls me every four-letter word in the book; I think he even created a few. It's show time!

Buddy calls for a backup because we know that this thing is escalating and we'll need a radio car to transport this nut to the precinct. I open the car door and Buddy and I start pulling this guy out of the car. He's not resisting, but he's not helping in any way, either. The guy just keeps coming out of the car; he's got to be 6'7" to 6'9". It's like one of those acts in the circus where the clowns keep coming out of the Volkswagen. But he's the only clown—and he's huge!

The cars are lining up behind us and horns are blowing and people are yelling. I figure, any second now some idiot is going to try to help this guy and all hell will break loose. I hear sirens approaching. Good sound.

Once I get this titan on the ground I try to put cuffs on him—and that's when he figures it's time to fight. But that's not going to happen, because this guy is just too big to punch it out with. So I reach for my nightstick and in true Police Academy style I start jabbing this guy with it in the torso, as Buddy and I try to get the cuffs on. He's thrashing around, but I seem to be in control as more TPF cops arrive and assist us.

Finally, we drag this guy into a radio car and Buddy drives the lunatic's car back to the precinct. I walk him inside the 71st Precinct and advise the desk officer of the charges. I then take him to the back room where I'll process the paperwork that accompanies the arrest.

I cuff him to a heavy metal chair and walk a few steps away to pick up the arrest cards. All of a sudden I hear this noise and the guy is full of blood. He lifted the chair on his back and ran headfirst into a radiator on the other side of the room. He starts screaming, "Police brutality, police brutality! I want my lawyer." The desk officer witnessed the entire scene and so did some civilians who were in the precinct at the time.

Now I have to take this psycho to Kings County Hospital for medical attention. That's where we meet his nattily dressed attorney who proceeds to scream that TPF cops are Nazis, along with other inflammatory remarks. As this arrogant attorney got in my face, I considered collaring him for harassment and obstructing governmental administration but thought better of it. All I need now is to lock up this lawyer and be proven wrong. I'm still on probation and could be fired for making such a mistake. So I bite my tongue and get the whacko his medical care before we return to the precinct and get this guy lodged in some holding cell for the night. Tomorrow he and his loudmouth lawyer will appear in Brooklyn Criminal Court. Ultimately, the mope will take a plea and the lawyer will get his fee, along with bragging rights that go with defending his "innocent" defendant against the "TPF Gestapo," which seemed to be his favorite description of our unit.

But it doesn't end here. The psycho had the temerity to file a civilian complaint against Buddy and me for brutality and theft. Yes, theft. The bum charged that Buddy, when searching the defendant's vehicle, ripped out a valuable stereo set and stole it. The whole thing was preposterous!

Both of us had to appear before an investigating sergeant who tape-recorded our versions of the story. We were nervous wrecks, worrying that this could, in some way, be used against us during our probationary period.

The complaint against us was dismissed, and to this day I am grateful that civilians happened to be in the precinct at the time and witnessed this nut's mad dash into the radiator. If it were not for them, then this could have come down to the madman's word against mine. And who knows what the outcome would have been?

There is no such thing as a simple car stop. All of these interventions have the potential to erupt into something unforeseen and bizarre and violent. Sometimes they can escalate into full-scale riots; the history of American policing is full of such case histories. Nothing is routine in police work.

Chapter 16
Grad School

While assigned to TPF I attended graduate school at night at John Jay College of Criminal Justice in Manhattan, where I pursued a master's degree in Criminal Justice. I had come to enjoy school, which was quite a turnaround from my days as an immature undergrad at St. John's University.

I had also come to realize that dropping out of St. John's was the right decision for me at the time. What appeared to be a totally illogical and immature decision actually turned out to be an important milestone in my life. Even today, I sometimes go against so-called traditional wisdom and counsel students that dropping out can be productive, if they understand the reasons for leaving school and then engage in a process to identify some goal that is important to them. The notion that dropping out is catastrophic and shameful is nonsense. There is a time and place to change course and determine if there is something else you want to do with your life. Dropping out and quitting, admittedly, is not always the preferred course of action, but it is an alternative that should be considered by those who temporarily get lost in the fog of life.

Graduate school was quite different from undergraduate classes. There were fewer class meetings, considerably more reading and more emphasis placed on writing research papers.

The police department was remarkably progressive about graduate education and permitted officers to change their tours of duty in order to attend classes. In effect, it meant that I could work day tours on Fridays and attend graduate classes in the evening. This was actually a new policy decision and I think it had to do with the fact that a number of cops pursuing graduate degrees were superior officers who had the political juice to get this policy carved into standard operating procedure. In any event, it worked for me and guaranteed that most Friday nights I would be hooking up with my friends by 10:30 P.M.

One Friday evening around 5:30 P.M., I strolled into John Jay College, which at the time was located on 24th Street and Park Avenue South in the Gramercy Park section of Manhattan, when a well-dressed, distinguished-looking, middle-aged man stopped me and asked me if I would have a cup of coffee with him. I recognized him as Assistant Chief Inspector Freddie Kowsky, a legendary figure in the history of the NYPD, who during the historic visit of Premier Nikita Khrushchev of the U.S.S.R. actually decked Khrushchev's bodyguard because he had the audacity to shove a cop. Freddie, a captain at the time, made the front page of *The Daily News* and became an overnight hero. He was the NYPD's answer to General Patton; he was a crusty, two-star warrior who lived for, and deeply loved, the police department.

You don't say "no" to a Chief, so I quickly joined Fred Kowsky, who bought the coffee and got right down to business. He told me that in a matter of days he would become Commanding Officer of the Special Operations Division, which included the Harbor and Aviation Units, the Motorcycle Precincts, Emergency Service Units and TPF, among other commands. The man literally ruled a force equivalent to some armies. The Chief told me that he wanted my feedback on TPF. "What do the troops want?" Freddie asked. "What can I do to help build morale?"

I was stunned that this veteran chief would ask me—a rookie with less than a year on the job—such an important question. But without batting an eye, I gave him my answer. "Chief, the men want lockers. We work out of our private cars, and travel around like a band of gypsies. We have no place to change, no place to call our own, so lockers would be the first thing the troops would want," I said to the chief, whose piercing eyes zeroed in on me.

Kowsky shook his head and then, as quickly as he started the conversation, he ended it by thanking me and telling me that if I ever needed anything, I should reach out to him directly. He gave me his office telephone number. We left the restaurant and both headed off to chain-smoking Professor Bill Wetteroth's class on *Police and the Community*, where Freddie spun colorful war stories to complement Bill's lectures.

I mentioned my encounter with Kowsky to Ronnie Risch, who then passed it along to some of the other guys. Some of the cops thought the whole thing was bullshit, that I was blowing smoke. Most of them probably thought that it was inconceivable that a chief would approach some wet-behind-the-ears rookie and seek his advice.

But two weeks after Kowsky took over TPF, the word came out that we were getting permanent lockers, that our days as nomads were over and that Chief Kowsky wanted to reward the unit for the fine work it had done over the years. Fred Kowsky had taught me a valuable lesson in leadership—"always take good care of the troops"—and he believed in this and he delivered the goods. My squad got lockers in the 4th Precinct on Varick Street in lower Manhattan, and there wasn't a man in TPF who wouldn't run through a brick wall for Chief Kowsky, the old war-horse.

All TPFers had nicknames, so I got tagged with "Graduate" by my squad, either in recognition of my curious status as a graduate student, or perhaps this sobriquet was based on the Dustin Hoffman's award-winning flick, "The Graduate," which captured the hilarious plights of an idealistic and naïve young man.

I think the vote was probably divided as to the origin of my nickname, but I liked it and thought it character-ized me pretty well. I'm still an unabashed idealist and damn proud to admit it. It beats being a cynic any day, for cynicism is a death knell in policing and in life in general.

Today I refer to myself as an idealistic realist. And I still like to watch "The Graduate" and "Patton." I take from both of these flicks that life should be filled with humor, and leaders should always take good care of the troops.

Chapter 17
Good Call

I had just completed a fairly uneventful 1800 x 0200 tour at the 6th Precinct, when I jumped into my '66 T-Bird and headed toward the Battery Tunnel, which would take me over to Brooklyn and on to my favorite watering hole called Jack's. I'd still have about an hour to hang out with the guys and toss a few brews before hitting the hay.

As I approached the two-lane tunnel a swerving car nearly sideswiped me and then the driver gassed it and sped into the entrance of the tunnel. I followed behind this moron because it was abundantly clear that this guy was drunk and dangerous. This was definitely an accident waiting to happen and odds were that the bum would hurt someone and peel off into the darkness.

Throughout the tunnel ride to Brooklyn the drunk driver repeatedly swerved across the yellow line and actually hit one of the sides of the tunnel and then caromed off. I stayed safely behind and straddled the middle line trying to keep other drivers from moving up on this guy and having a collision.

We make it to the other side and I decide that I'll stop this skell at the tollbooth. Think again. Yeah, this half-wit is really going to stop and pay a toll to some guy wearing a blue uniform. No way! So he guns his rusty, green Dodge and nearly clipped the startled toll collector, who immediately tried to get the guy's tag number. I follow behind, flash my shield to the toll collector and proceed to follow this guy off the Hamilton Avenue Exit, which is the first one in Brooklyn.

A few blocks from the tunnel I manage to pull this guy over; he surprisingly complies and edges his car over to the curb. As I get out of my car I'm trying to figure out what precinct I'm in and what is the best way of handling this off-duty arrest. The drunk gets out of his car and starts walking toward a brick wall, all the time ignoring my orders to freeze and keep his hands where I can see them. As he gets closer to the wall, he turns toward me and reaches for what I know has to be a gun. The right hand is reaching across his belt buckle moving quickly toward his left hip and I know he's coming out with a piece. By this time I'm exposed; I no longer have the cover of either vehicle and so I crouch and go for my weapon. All the time now, I am screaming and calling this bastard every four-letter word I can imagine. I take a combat stance and am ready to squeeze the trigger, when I see his right hand whipping out of his belt area—but there is no gun. I'm totally confused. There is no way another human being—even a drunk, irrational one—is going to make believe he's drawing on a cop who in fact has a gun and is ready to blow him off the face of the earth. I charge him like I'm completely out of my mind and I drive him as hard as I can into the brick wall. He smiles and goes limp. "Where's the gun, you bastard? Where is it?" I scream.

I pat the son-of-a-bitch down and then go over him more thoroughly. There must be a gun. Sirens approach from all sides of me. I have a crushing headache and this whole thing seems like a nightmare. The first radio car team arrives and I start yelling, "I'm on the job! On the job!" I hold my shield up and rotate it so that the cops responding from all directions can see it. All I need now is to get blown away by another cop while in the process of making an *off-duty* DWI collar. The uniformed guys, now about six in number, help me up and take control of the prisoner, who still has this idiotic smile on his face.

I tell one of the cops what happened and he immediately goes to the skell's car where he's certain he'll find the gun. But there is no gun! So either this bastard thought he had his piece with him, or he lost his gun after a night of partying, or he wanted me to blow him away. Maybe this guy wanted to die at the hands of a cop. Maybe it was his way to end it all. Maybe I was to be his instrument of death.

I actually believe that he thought he had his gun with him that night in Red Hook. The guy took a position that indicated to me that he knew how to draw a weapon and that he was all set to do so. God only knows what would have happened if I had fired that night. I know in my heart and my mind and in my soul that I was justified in doing so. But what would a grand jury think of my actions? Would they think I had been reckless and could have avoided the entire affair in some fashion? Would they criticize me for taking this type of police action while off duty?

If I hadn't caught a glimpse of that empty hand in the dim illumination of the summer moon, I would have fired my weapon. And I would not have had any qualms about blowing that guy right off the face of the earth. If it's between another guy and me, then I'm coming out on top. He put himself in that position and he would pay the ultimate price for his mistake. As the saying goes, I'd rather be judged by twelve than carried by six.

Thank God, my split-second decision turned out to be right, but it could easily have gone the other way and my entire life would have been dramatically changed forever. Then again, my life may have ended if that drunken bastard had his gun with him that night.

Chapter 18
Partner for Life

I t had been a long Saturday night, so I decided to sleep in on Sunday morning. I usually hit two or three watering holes an evening; sometimes I traveled alone but mostly I bounced around with some of my friends, a few of whom were also cops. Some nights I would strike up a conversation with a girl and have a few drinks with her at the bar. This might lead to a date or two, but before long I was back out with my friends making the rounds. Actually, I was rather content being single and liked hanging around with my friends.

It had been a tough week at work because I had made two collars and spent a lot of time in court waiting for my cases to be called. After court, I would report to TPF for another 6:00 P.M. to 2:00 A.M. tour of duty and then would go home for a few hours of shuteye before heading back to court. So Sunday I figured I would just stay home and relax and maybe do some work on a term paper for my graduate course. It was February 22, 1970—Washington's Birthday.

Around 6 o'clock that evening the phone rang and it was Gerry Koban, my fireman friend who hung out with me at Jack's, my favorite bar and grill. Gerry, a redheaded firebrand with an upbeat attitude toward life, wanted me to go to dinner with him at a local restaurant. Afterward we would have a few drinks at the bar and then call it an early night and head home. I told Gerry that I was spent, that I had this paper I was working on and just wasn't up for another night out. Gerry was persistent and he wore me down, so I threw on a sports jacket and a tie and met Gerry at Griswold's Pub, which was only half a mile from my apartment.

During dinner, Gerry and I covered our usual array of topics: politics and war stories in both the Fire Department and the Police Department; his steady girl, Kathy, with whom he had just had an argument; and our plans for next weekend, which always depended on coordinating our work charts. After dinner, as we stepped out to the bar area, Gerry yelled out, "Patricia, what the hell are you doing here?"

I looked toward this Patricia and stopped dead in my tracks; the proverbial lightning struck, I started to sweat and instantly I knew my face was flushed. I had never had such a reaction to a girl. Pat was drop-dead gorgeous. I was speechless and completely unnerved. Gerry, realizing that his friend looked like he was having some kind of seizure, immediately introduced me to this Pat. She was with three other girls, but I never looked their way, even when Gerry introduced me to them.

Pat was petite and shapely; she had long auburn hair, stunning hazel eyes, stood 5'1½", and had an engaging smile. I made small talk with her, of which I have absolutely no recollection because I was trying not to hyperventilate, stammer and blow the whole evening. Gerry kept chatting on about one inane thing or another and tried to help relax me because he knew that I had been hooked. The other girls turned out to be Pat's sister, Kathy, her best friend Delia, and another friend who complimented me on my colorful tie by constantly shouting a four-letter word with great enthusiasm to demonstrate her approval of my choice of neckwear. I wanted to crawl in a hole.

Once I remembered how to form some coherent sentences, Pat and I talked for two hours; she seemed to have some interest in me. But the garrulous Gerry, who was as subtle as a raging bull in a china shop, announced that I was a college graduate, that I was going to be police commissioner someday, and that I drove a '66 T-Bird. At one point I wanted to choke him, but I could see that Pat knew Gerry for years and she just smiled at his feeble attempt to make me seem like Prince Charming. She wanted me to know that I shouldn't be embarrassed. Pat had a nice way about her.

The night was coming to a quick close so I garnered up enough courage to ask for Pat's telephone number, which she unhesitatingly gave me. We met on Wednesday and Friday and had a good time together. Then on Saturday we went out on our first so-called formal date at a place called The Tankard Inn. The hours flew by and we went out the next night and every night I wasn't working right up to April 17th, when I gave Pat an engagement ring. Five weeks later on May 23rd we were married at Our Lady of Perpetual Help Church. We had seriously considered eloping, but in deference to our parents and to keep the family peace, we did the whole wedding extravaganza and were joined by over 200 friends and relatives at our reception. All of this happened over a period of 90 days.

After a three-day honeymoon in the Poconos, we moved into our one-bedroom apartment on Shore Road that we rented for $175, which was more than we could afford at the time. But we got by. We always do.

On February 4, 1971, Pat gave birth to our son, Thomas, who decided to arrive a few weeks early. Light on birth weight but strong of character our baby boy changed our lives and undoubtedly was the best thing ever to happen to us.

━━━━━━━━━━━━━━━━━━━━━━━━━━━

Pat and I just celebrated our 32nd Anniversary, all because an insistent Gerry Koban convinced me to go to dinner with him over three decades ago. About eleven years ago, Gerry retired from the Fire Department as a Captain, after battling blazes and selflessly helping people for twenty-two years. Just recently, after a year-long battle fought with great dignity and courage, Gerry succumbed to cancer at the age of 54. Up until the very end, he exhibited an indomitable spirit and a self-deprecating sense of humor. Even during those final days when he had a tough go of it with chemotherapy, he'd take my phone calls and we'd reminisce about the "good ole days." Gerry will always be in our thoughts and prayers, for he was a wonderful friend and certainly one of New York's Bravest.

Chapter 19
Undercover

My graduate education continued one night when, after a particularly uninspiring lecture, I was approached by a Detective Captain who wanted to speak with me. Right off the bat, the Captain wanted to know if I would be interested in being assigned to the Detective Division. This question is equivalent to being asked if you want to accept your multimillion dollar lottery prize. The question was so bizarre that I actually thought that this was some kind of stunt being pulled by someone in the class. But it was not.

The Captain was seeking someone young to go undercover to investigate large-scale employee pilferage in the newspaper industry. Put simply, employees were stealing over $2 million in newspapers each year, and the company believed its viability was in question if the internal theft problem continued. These employees had essentially set up their own companies by selling stolen newspapers—yes, newspapers, which they sold on a black market at reduced prices. The assignment would be a blue-collar job and I had some experience working as a laborer on the Brooklyn waterfront loading and unloading cargo, so that helped. Besides that, it was thought that a college student would play nicely into the case because as a shape-up employee, who had to show up at a hiring pool each evening, I could say that I needed the dough to pay for college.

The Captain arranged an interview and within days—of what seemed to be a *pro forma* meeting—I was transferred to the Detective Division "forthwith," as they say in police parlance. With just over a year and a half in uniform I had reached my first goal—assignment to the Detective Division. Networking in grad school was becoming my vehicle for success in the NYPD.

Many of my colleagues in TPF were stunned, but they were happy for me and generous in wishing me well. TPF represented a special breed in the NYPD and I don't think it's an overstatement that at a TPF reunion a few years ago someone sold golf shirts with the inscription, *"Our like will not be seen again" 1959 to 1984.* The shirts were sold out in minutes and I think this demonstrated our fraternal pride in serving in one of the most effective and elite units ever to be assembled in the history of the New York City Police Department. I have always been resentful that the department saw fit to abolish this top-notch outfit during its Silver Anniversary Year. I felt, and still do, that this action was unwarranted and demonstrated little respect for the troops who frequently kept New York City from coming apart at the seams during tense civil disorders. TPF had its detractors, but when the City needed to quell a problem, the first guys sent in all had the letters TPF on their collars. Some of the finest cops I have known served in the Tactical Patrol Force at one point in their careers.

As crazy as this may seem today, thirty years ago there was absolutely no training provided for under-covers. You were in uniform one day, and the next day you were to assume your new identity, using your best theatrical skills, a good sense of humor, and always ever conscious of being fast on your feet by having answers to all questions. Piece of cake.

Former FBI Special Agent Jim Abbott tells of the time that he was asked to join his criminal associates at a swimming pool on a scorching day in Puerto Rico. Abbott, who was working on an organized crime case and wired, was wearing a three-piece suit and had to convince his fellow swimmers that his flowing perspiration was the result of the flu and that he didn't want to get worse by jumping in the pool. Thank God, the wiseguys went for it hook, line and sinker. Jim Abbott got to live, for discovery of that wire in the back hills of Puerto Rico would have meant certain death for this quick-thinking, hero agent.

Abbott, who now serves as Deputy Commissioner of the Suffolk County Police Department on Long Island, suffered severe health-related problems as a result of his undercover assignment. Consequently, he has become a strong proponent for establishing training and counseling programs for law enforcement officers who work undercover assignments. Jim encouraged the FBI to establish a formal training program for undercovers at the FBI Academy in Quantico, Virginia. He also serves as an adjunct professor at St. John's University, where one can hear a pin drop during Jim's powerful and heartfelt lectures to future police officers.

Now my undercover role was in no way as perilous as Jim Abbott's was—not nearly. But, it's worth pointing out that the transformation from uniformed officer to undercover requires much more preparation, both tactical and psychological, than what departments provided in the past, which was essentially nothing. For instance, I was told that I was to be particularly careful of being followed home from work, because my superiors had some information that new employees were sometimes tailed to see if they were cops. Fine, that's understandable. But no one gave me untraceable license plates to put on my *personal* vehicle, which I was required to use to get to and from work. That is downright stupid. First, you hype me up about a tail, which never happened by the way, and then in the same breath you tell me that you can't give me a car or even plates that are not traceable back to my residence. All the bad guy had to do was copy down my plate number. You didn't have to follow me, for my plates told the story of where I lived—and bad guys know how to trace plates. Why the hell didn't they just give us marked radio cars?

The days of enlightenment, however, had not yet arrived for undercovers in the law enforcement world. Thanks to courageous leaders like Jim Abbott, things are a lot better today for those who choose to accept undercover assignments. The screening process is much more methodical and comprehensive, and the training addresses the psychological, physical and emotional effects of undercover work, which over time can place tremendous stress on the person. Just ask Jim Abbott, who, over the course of his undercover assignment, gained considerable weight and experienced a number of serious health problems, which he believes were attributable to the stress caused by his undercover assignment.

One of the things that undercovers can experience is an identity crisis. Undercovers lead two separate lives. One that is based on a complete lie, and another that is grounded in ordinary familial relationships. Now, that in itself is an inherent conflict of enormous magnitude.

One day, after having become fed up with the slow pace of the investigation and not enjoying my new look, which sported long hair and a greasy beard, I went to a barber and got all cleaned up. I told the barber to return me to my preppie look. Well, I got rave reviews from my wife.

As you would guess, however, my boss went haywire, even though I knew that I could still pull off my act without the traditional undercover look. I had complete confidence in myself and knew that my new look would eliminate any suspicions anyone might have had about me. Think about it, the bad guys had to figure that I was definitely not an undercover because it made absolutely no sense to take on the stereotypical appearance of a cop if, in fact, I was a police officer. This convoluted thinking along with the handy excuse that I cleaned up because I had to go for a job interview, solidified my position as an undercover.

The undercover assignment lacked the excitement of a typical tour of duty in TPF. Besides, the solitary nature of an undercover's role made me feel disengaged from real police work and the NYPD. The case handlers actually told me to tell other cops that I didn't work in the unit where I was assigned, when the entire department could just look at transfer orders and see that I had been assigned to a specific squad in the Detective Division. These guys wanted this case to be something it certainly was not, and they had some Hollywood notion of how to manage an undercover operation. In my estimation, their approach and strategy didn't comport with reality, and in short order, I got real bored with the operation and the cast of characters who supported it.

But then I had what I considered to be a brilliant idea. This got my juices flowing again. I called Ronnie Risch, who had been my best man at our wedding, and told him about my proposed caper. He promptly told me that I was out of my goddamn mind and that I shouldn't call him back until I was sober. Twenty minutes later, having put the final touches on my proposed escapade, I called Risch and convinced him that within 48 hours he would be assigned to the Detective Division—with me as his partner. I would now use my best undercover and acting skills to make this case interesting.

I told Ronnie to meet me in a local diner and as soon as he walked in the door, he went ballistic when he saw my new look. "Have you lost your goddamn mind? What the hell made you do this? And now you're telling me that you are having me transferred to the Detective Division?"

Two elderly ladies shot us glares and we toned down a bit before I would tell Ronnie about my Master Plan.

But before I unfurled my scheme, we ordered bacon and eggs, with Risch telling the waitress no less than three times to "burn" the bacon. Once again, the old ladies looked our way. I lowered my eyes in embarrassment. But Risch just kept harping on about me being *loco*. And this is before I tell him about my plan. When the bacon arrived, which looked like a charred tongue depressor, he sent it back—it wasn't burnt enough. And he calls me *loco!*

I called the Assistant District Attorney assigned to the newspaper case a few minutes before 9:00 A.M. The ADA was a creature of habit and he'd be arriving at his desk right about this time.

"It's Tom. We got a problem, but I took care of it." I didn't stop talking; I wanted to cover every critical point before he even had a chance to ask a question.

"Look, I had to tell the guy. We worked together in TPF and I had no choice but to tell him. He's a stand-up guy, so there'll be no problems with any leaks," I explained to the ADA, who was known to be a little hyper.

After I calmed the ADA down a bit, he told me to reach out to Ronnie and bring him to the office as soon as I could.

I got Risch on the line and told him to meet me in a coffee shop across from the DA's office in an hour. So far, things were going according to Hoyle.

Risch darts into the coffee shop and I wave him over. Right away, I can see the guy is a nervous wreck; I had never seen him so anxious.

"Ronnie, everything's fine. Just stick to your story and the whole tale has a happy ending," I assure him.

A happy ending? Risch starts to get off on one of his diatribes when I cut him short and tell him that I guarantee the outcome. Risch just shakes his head, but

I can tell that he likes this living on the edge as much, or more, than I do, so down deep he's enjoying himself in some perverse way that goes along with the uncertainty and danger of being a cop.

The ADA meets with both of us and Risch explains how he walked into the newspaper plant, which is near his girlfriend's house, to use the men's room and he ran right into me. Ronnie goes on to tell the ADA what a great job I did by moving Ronnie away from the people in the plant, so I could tip him off that I wasn't moonlighting but working undercover. Risch plays the part perfectly and I can see that the ADA already likes Ronnie who's playing it humble. He's a damned good actor.

The ADA asks me to step outside with him for a moment. He wants to know what I know about this guy, his reputation, his work habits, etc. I tell him the guy had a sterling reputation in TPF. I don't volunteer that we were steady partners, that he's my best man, that he's godfather to my son, that we hang out together and that we're now co-conspirators in this plot to reunite as partners. I use my best altar boy face to sell this deal.

Ronnie Risch joined me in my undercover escapades and he literally thrived in that environment; the guy was a natural. He was like a chameleon: he blended into the environment and had the uncanny ability to take on different identities and alter his approach at the drop of a dime. Ronnie has natural acting skills and a razor sharp sense of humor. And besides that, he could drive a truck with a manual transmission, which I couldn't. Ronnie tried to teach me to drive a newspaper delivery truck, but this resulted in my driving up on a sidewalk and almost taking out six parked cars and some guy's new chain link fence.

Once Ronnie was firmly established as an undercover we went about putting together a case that resulted in over 80 arrests. The massive employee pilferage that had plagued this industry for years came to a screeching halt as the press obviously played up this case, which was aimed at deterring others from engaging in such behavior.

One of the guys collared in this case said that he was "shocked" that he had been arrested. He felt that he should have been warned first. "For Christ sakes," he said, "we're being treated like real criminals. Don't the cops have anything else to do? Stealing newspapers? The politicians are walking away with the whole city and I get nabbed for stealing a few papers," the guy lamented as he waited in a holding cell for arraignment. Then he turned to me and said, "How d'hell you get out so fast?" I just smiled at him and flashed my shield.

"Hey, kid, where'd you get that goddamn badge? It looks real."

I knew I could pull this off—even with my preppie look!

Chapter 20
Wiseguys

O nce we wrapped up the newspaper case, I was assigned to the Rackets Bureau, which concentrated its investigative efforts on organized crime. New York City's five crime families were in their heyday and Don Carlo Gambino reigned supreme as head of the mob's Commission. The primary weapons used against organized crime were electronic eavesdropping and surveillance and, of course, informants who look to cut the best deal they can with prosecutors—despite their professed fidelity to the *Code of Omerta*. For a young cop this was heady work; you got to see who the wiseguys were and how they operated, which wasn't very smart.

Let me give you an example. I would monitor wiretaps and listen in on the conversations that occurred between gangsters. Invariably, these mopes would say something along the lines that the phones "are up," so don't say anything of importance or of an incriminating nature. Moments later, they would go ahead and say precisely something that was of importance to us. One day, two "made guys" are talking about a meeting that would be of interest to us because we were carefully tracking the mob's influence and control of the private sanitation industry. They were particularly careful not to give away the time, date and location of the meeting, each time reminding themselves that the "bastards are probably listening, so don't say nothing." This happened a few times and as these grammarians were wrapping up, I felt that the conversation was a useless recording of supposed "hot tips" from degenerate gamblers, the names of waitresses who did more than serve food, and the latest weather report from mob central. But then as one moron is getting ready to hang up, he blurts out, "Yeah, I'll see you 7 o'clock at Jilly's," and then he hangs up the phone. Immediately the boss put together a male and female team of detectives who posed as lovers out for an evening at this Manhattan restaurant. The cops managed to position themselves close enough to the wise guys' table so that they were able to overhear a vital conversation that helped us with the case. All of this happened because the mope let down his guard as he was hanging up the phone. There were countless examples of similar type comments flowing from the mouths of these scholars, almost instantly after reminding themselves that the cops were probably listening in on their conversations. It never failed to amaze me how self-destructive these thugs could be. Equally amazing to me was why law enforcement was incapable of putting these bums out of business.

Another quick story about the mob and rats—but not the type that squeals on other wiseguys. This time I'm talking about rodents. One night I'm assigned to monitor an eavesdropping bug that has been installed in the ceiling of a mob-operated social club. I hook up with another cop from the Public Morals Administrative Division (PMAD), a guy I have never met before. I meet this cop in the basement of a decrepit warehouse where we will listen in on any conversations coming out of the club. It's a Sunday evening, so no one is at the club and the bug is dead silent. After chatting with the PMAD cop for a few hours, we decide to catch some shuteye since the silence is deafening and it appears that no one is going to show up at the social club tonight. The PMAD cop takes a position on a beat-up, old couch and I sit in an equally run-down recliner and push it back to its full reclining position. All the comforts of home this is not. But we'll make do.

Both of us will hear the bug should any of the wise-guys choose to come to the club for a meet. But as far as we know, no one has yet to visit on a Sunday and the bug has been in for some time now.

We are dozing off when I hear a siren noise coming over the bug, and the sound gets progressively louder. I open my eyes and move the recliner to the sitting position when, all of sudden, I see an enormous rat falling on top of the other cop; it had jumped or fallen from the rafters. The cop is just opening his eyes as the rat lands right on his arm. The guy is panic-stricken and throws his arm up defensively and the rat flies off and heads through the air towards me. The cop has propelled this huge rat toward me as I sit there taking in this whole scene. Now, to make matters worse, if that's possible, the cop now has his gun trained right on me. Evidently, when he closed his eyes, he held his revolver in his right hand and crossed his arms across his chest. The rat landed on his right arm and, when he violently flung the rodent off his arm and toward me, the weapon followed. Now I have an airborne rat coming my way as I look down the barrel of this guy's gun. I was paralyzed with fear. What the hell could I do? Thank God, the rat fell just short of landing on me and scampered off, as the cop, now fully awake from his nightmare, lowered the gun.

Needless to say, we never closed our eyes again that evening or at any other time. I hate rats and I was miffed that the NYPD always found the most God-awful places on earth to have us monitor wires and bugs. I'd rather deal with a Mafia rat any day; just keep me away from the ones with the four legs and long tails. Rats make my skin crawl.

Apparently a fire engine responded to a deli right next door to the social club. The siren must have spooked the rat and triggered this unimaginable series of events.

Just another false alarm for the FDNY, but for us this was the real thing.

I often wondered how the police department would explain to Pat that another cop, who had just propelled a huge rat at your husband, had then shot him—and the whole thing was just a big mistake? What an undistinguished way to earn a Full Inspector's Funeral! Again, Lady Luck saw fit to be with me, as I unwittingly got myself in the middle of a scene that even Chief Inspector Clouseau could not have concocted.

Chapter 21
Mob Hit

O ne day I was directed to report to Columbus Circle in Manhattan where Joe Colombo, the head of the crime family carrying his name, would hold a rally of the Italian-American Civil Rights League. Colombo had gone against the wishes of the old Mustache Petes—the traditional Mafia dons who held that *La Cosa Nostra* was something that never took on a public face in any fashion—and he created a nonprofit organization ostensibly to combat discrimination against Italian-Americans. Colombo even went so far as to picket the FBI headquarters in Manhattan.

I report to an intersection near Columbus Circle, which is adjacent to Manhattan's Central Park, where a detective sergeant tells us our specific assignments. The sergeant also hands out lapel buttons that indicate the agency we represent. This was to be a joint federal, state and local initiative, since any agency that had juris-diction in the area of organized crime, wants to be at the rally to collect intelligence information and snap some updated photos of Colombo Family "made men" and associates.

The sergeant tells us we have time to get a bite to eat before the rally would begin, so along with another cop I head for a coffee shop. My specific assignment will be to mill around the assembled crowd and show the flag, so to speak. We are there to monitor the wiseguys and arrest any mope we recognize who is wanted and has the audacity and stupidity to show up at the rally. I order some coffee and pie and shoot the breeze before heading over to Columbus Circle, well in advance of the noon start time.

I stroll around the perimeter of the rally site and then walk toward the stage area where none other than Joe Colombo himself is getting ready for the big show—his big show. I glance at Colombo who smiles and nods his head.

As I turn to walk away from the stage area shots ring out. I reach for my weapon because these shots are close to me. A tall, uniformed cop pushes me to the ground as I yell, "I'm on the job! On the job!" Apparently, he saw me go for my gun and didn't know whether I was a cop or a bad guy. Confusion reigns supreme as I get up and move toward a black guy who is down on the ground and bleeding. In front of this guy lies a camera.

To my right, another guy is being lifted into an ambulance that had been parked near the stage; two women nearby are hysterical. The guy being placed into the ambulance is bleeding from his mouth, nose and ears. He's obviously in bad shape.

A priest jumps up on the stage and emotionally requests prayers for Joey. And then it hits me like a ton of bricks. The dead, black guy shot Colombo and then someone whacked the shooter. All in a matter of seconds. All in front of so many cops and agents and yet—so far—there doesn't seem to be an actual eyewitness to what had taken place in broad daylight, in the middle of Manhattan.

Apparently, the black guy, whose name would turn out to be Jerome Johnson, had pretended to be a photographer and had asked Colombo for a picture, when out comes a gun, down goes the camera and Colombo is shot in the head. Instantaneously, the mob's button man shoots Johnson and somehow the hit man manages to get out of the area and—as far as I know—is still unidentified. To this day, the case remains unsolved.

More people now arrive for the rally and the crowd becomes more agitated as they hear the story of the shooting. Cops round up known wiseguys and whisk them off to the local precinct, where paraffin tests are conducted to see if there is any gunpowder residue on their hands. Some blacks strolling through the area are set upon by angry rally participants; these fools now want to blame all blacks for the shooting of their leader.

Police commanders of every conceivable rank arrive at the scene of the shooting, and yet no one actually knows what went down. The heads of the five families and their high command are rounded up over the next few hours and interrogated in an attempt to find out what this is all about, before the inevitable mob war starts.

Out of all this violence and confusion comes forth a theory that Joey Gallo, a famous and eccentric wiseguy from Brooklyn, while in a state penitentiary convinces Jerome Johnson, another inmate, to shoot Joe Colombo in exchange for a lifetime of financial security. It is thought that Gallo convinced the highly suggestible, and probably deranged Johnson, that he would be taken care of for life, and that he would be whisked out of the area and not apprehended because Gallo had devised a fool-proof escape plan.

Another version has it that Gallo convinced Johnson he would be wounded superficially and then placed in the ambulance at the side of the stage and driven off to some hiding place, where he would recuperate from his wounds and then live a life of riches. The gullible Johnson was not told that his wounds would be fatal and that he would be dead by the time he hit the sidewalk.

This was an assassination attempt that was almost perfect in its execution, except that Joe Colombo did not die immediately and lived in a comatose state for another seven years.

For his alleged role in the plot, Joey Gallo would later be gunned down in Umberto's Clam House in Manhattan's Little Italy. Gallo brought heat on the mob much in the same way that Colombo did by his efforts to go public and embarrass the FBI. The mob world, not unlike life in general, has its ironies.

My wife Pat heard about the shooting on the radio and knew I was there because I had called her from the coffee shop before reporting to Columbus Circle. When I got the opportunity, I gave her a call and I could sense her distress as she asked me if I had been near the shooting. Knowing my uncanny ability to be right in the middle of trouble, she intuitively knew that I had to be somewhere in the mix. This wouldn't be the last time I would be at a famous shooting.

Chapter 22
Mob Hit and Miss

O ne of the most fascinating stories I heard about the mob had to do with a smalltime wiseguy who kept getting locked up by different law enforcement agencies in the City of New York. This guy, somewhere in his 30s, evidently was a colossal moron and just couldn't avoid getting collared. Now when this happens, the mob guys get worried; they think right away that the guy will become a rat to cut some time off his sentence. But this guy, albeit inept and stupid, was not a rat.

One night, this gangster is told to report to a restaurant after closing, to see his *capo*. The guy goes to the restaurant and after dinner the *capo*—just like in the movies—kisses him on the cheek as another mob guy pulls out a handgun and fires two .22 rounds into the guy's head. The shooter and his accomplice start to shove the victim into a plastic bag when, all of a sudden, the guy regains consciousness and breaks loose from the bag and runs right through a plate glass window and lands on the sidewalk. Now, it doesn't end here. The guy runs down the block and is seen by police officers in a passing radio car; the cops take the guy to the hospital where he makes a dying declaration, telling exactly what happened and who shot him.

From an evidentiary perspective, the dying declaration is worth its weight in gold, so the shooter and his accomplice are arrested. Under the laws of evidence, it is reasoned that the person making such a declaration believes he is going to die imminently, so he has little reason to lie since he is about to meet his Maker. A dying declaration can place someone on death row.

But what do you think happens on the way to the courthouse? The wiseguy who took two bullets to the head, which by some minor miracle circumvented his cranium but did not puncture his brain, recants his dying declaration and says the whole thing is some mistake. And he refuses to testify. I have no idea what ever happened to this guy, but for one thing I know, he wasn't a rat—and for once in his miserable life he was lucky—if you can call this luck. You just can't make up stories like this. And I guess that is why Hollywood loves the mob so much.

I tried to convince this guy that he should testify against the wiseguys, that he was never going to be safe again if he didn't enter the Witness Protection Program. The guy, a chain smoker, flatly refused to testify and had this terrified look frozen on his face that was punctuated by a pronounced facial twitch. After talking to this guy for an hour, I started to twitch.

By the end of that day, I was left with one thought that stays with me to this day. The wiseguy life has no honor, no glamour and is staffed by dissolute lowlifes who should be eradicated from the face of the earth—with due process, of course. And yes, I think that this can be done!

The Godfather with its artful writing, superb acting and creative cinematography essentially glorifies the mob. But *Goodfellas,* with its unexaggerated violence and its outstanding cast, portrays the Mafia the way it really is in American popular culture.

Chapter 23
Moving On

O ne of my problems is that I get bored quickly and want to seek out new experiences. Even though I was now assigned to the Detective Division and was in line to receive the coveted gold shield of a New York City Detective, I was not content.

I had received an offer to become an instructor at the Police Academy and was thinking seriously of accepting that faculty position. I had always liked the idea of being in the classroom, so this assignment appealed to me and it was widely known that Academy instructors climbed the ranks quickly because they were more familiar with the academic materials that served as the basis for civil service promotional exams.

Frankly, I thought that my investigative unit could take a much more aggressive stance against crime and was disappointed in the amount of downtime involved in criminal investigations. There is no doubt that an investigator must be painstakingly patient, but even then I knew that there was something wrong with our almost casual approach to crime suppression.

I had come from TPF where we were used to an aggressive approach to combat street crime; every night there was a sense of adventure as we hit the streets and hunted down the bad guys. The TPF approach was strikingly fundamental, but the results were extraordinary.

Edward Norris, who is the Police Commissioner of Baltimore and a former Deputy Commissioner for Operations at the NYPD, perhaps best captures the state of crime fighting before the "police management revolution" occurred in the mid 1990s. "The NYPD was flying with blinders on," Norris states emphatically to demonstrate the unfocused and ineffective approach that had become standard operating procedure for New York's Finest.

In my assignment in the Detective Division I felt like an insignificant cog in an inefficient investigative machine. I became increasingly frustrated that assistant district attorneys ran the investigations from A to Z in my unit; there was little discretion left for the investigator. And I was bored stiff!

I was also disappointed in the fact that the civil service promotional process in the NYPD was lengthy and favored those with seniority. Admittedly, I was ambitious and impatient and wanted to get into some supervisory role as quickly as possible. Patience is not my strong suit. Never has been.

I was now at a crossroads and had to make a decision.

A college classmate of mine, Dick Ward, had just accepted a position as an Assistant Dean at John Jay College of Criminal Justice and so I thought I would visit him and get his take on my situation. Dick had been a New York City Detective and had won a fellowship to the University of California at Berkeley where he had recently earned a doctorate in criminology. I valued Dick's advice and arranged to have lunch with my friend.

I left that lunch more confused than ever. Dick informed me that John Jay was looking for a Director of Security and he wanted to know if I would be a candidate for this newly created position. Dick indicated that I was a perfect match for this job. I had patrol and investigative experience; I knew the players at the college; and I was young enough to relate to both the cops who attended the college and to the full-time students coming right out of high school who wanted careers in law enforcement. My lack of knowledge about physical security could be overcome by enrolling in the

Police Academy's Crime Prevention course. Dick had it all figured out. He also said that I could probably teach as an adjunct professor once I got my feet wet as the security director.

Dick said he couldn't promise anything, but he felt that the college president would support his recommendation to hire me. To make matters even more confusing, the job would more than double the salary I was earning as a New York City cop. This would be a no-brainer for many cops, but to leave the NYPD would be a major career move and one I had to give some serious thought to before being enticed by the bigger bucks.

Now there were three alternatives to consider: stay where I was and await my gold shield; transfer to the Police Academy; or, accept the position at John Jay College. Life was becoming either more charmed or more difficult. The whole thing had become more complicated than I ever imagined.

Pat said she would support any decision I made, but I sensed that she would not shed any tears if I left policing behind me. Spouses dread the ring of the doorbell and the sight of the uniformed officer and chaplain who are there to inform them that their loved ones were injured or died in the line of duty. And now that we had a baby, the John Jay position presented an opportunity to have a more routinized family life.

The idea of running my own security department and teaching at John Jay College of Criminal Justice got my juices flowing. I had pursued my master's degree because I wanted to prepare myself for a management position in law enforcement and also to teach at the university level. Now I would have my chance to do both—and at the same time.

I turned in my gun and shield and bought a tweed sports jacket, a blue blazer and some button-down shirts. I now had a new uniform of the day.

Chapter 24
Risky Business

R esigning from the NYPD was less difficult than I thought it would be. Actually, it was made easier by the fact that I could return to the department within a year if I were able to pass a medical exam, which I didn't think would present a problem. So in a way I was on a leave of absence and that made the resignation far less difficult, since I now had a safety net in case I had this strong desire to return to the NYPD, or if I didn't like my new position, or if my new employer didn't like my performance.

Since I would start this new department from scratch, I decided that John Jay College of Criminal Justice had a built-in resource for staffing its security function. This resource was its full-time students who aspired to careers in the criminal justice system as police officers, probation and parole personnel, federal investigators and other positions in the justice system. In short order, I hired over one hundred students on a part-time basis, trained them, had them don navy blue blazers with the department logo embroidered on the breast pocket, and then deployed them around-the-clock at our two campus buildings. The experiment worked like a charm and received media attention and a feature article in *The New York Daily News*.

Next, I learned all I could about alarm systems and then wrote the technical specifications for a fairly elaborate security system, which would be monitored by our student patrol force. Professor Bob Hair, who was John Jay's in-house expert on security systems and a retired Deputy Inspector from the NYPD, assisted me in this task. Things were falling in place and I liked the idea of being in charge of something and using creativity and leadership to resolve problems.

I quickly put an end to a ring of burglars who stole valuable textbooks from faculty offices and then sold them at local bookstores. The faculty and administration applauded our early success at crime fighting, and I was having a ball running my own show.

The next phase of my plan involved a major risk and one that raised a few eyebrows. I decided to hire as student security officers some ex-offenders recently released from Rikers Island. John Jay had a successful program at Rikers Island for inmates who wanted to begin their college education before they returned to their communities. During the 1970s, there had been a greater emphasis placed on inmate rehabilitation programs and a number of colleges throughout the nation were involved in these educational initiatives. But no one was putting these ex-cons to work as security officers.

A friend of mine didn't mince words in reacting to my idea: "Are you nuts? You're going to give the keys to John Jay College to a bunch of inmates just released from Rikers Island?"

Well, the answer was a qualified yes. But it would not be a bunch of prisoners—just a few at a time. The applicants would be carefully screened, interviewed and investigated, to determine their risk of recidivism. And, of course, they would be closely monitored. I was willing to take a risk, but I wasn't going to shoot myself in the foot and put an end to my new career before it had a chance to begin.

The first ex-offender hired was Claude Walton, a 6'4" black Korean War veteran who had spent a good portion of his adult life in prison for property-related crimes. Claude knew what the scoop was; he knew he would be watched closely and he was perceptive enough to know that some people wanted him to fail. Claude had a lifetime of failures, so this time he was determined to succeed.

Claude quickly moved through the ranks of the security department and his integrity was never questioned. I had the great pleasure of appointing him to the position of Assistant Director of Security, and the expression on Claude's face when I told him about his promotion will stay with me for the rest of my life.

Claude Walton was a special human being; he served John Jay College with distinction for many years and as a tribute for his extraordinary service, his name appears on a memorial plaque reserved for those deceased faculty members and administrators who made distinguished contributions to the college

Claude Walton was absolutely loyal to me and I trusted him completely. My life became richer as a result of knowing this gentle giant of a man who I truly believed lacked but one thing in life—an opportunity. Once he got it, he excelled and reached his potential.

The experiment also had some failures. A few ex-offenders turned out to be con men who betrayed the trust we placed in them and they were terminated. But on balance, I believe this ex-offender educational and employment program worked well.

The program certainly contributed to my understanding of correctional philosophies that place greater emphasis on community treatment modalities, as opposed to "lock 'em up and throw away the key" approaches. Later in life this new knowledge would be helpful to me, when I became Assistant Commissioner of the New York City Department of Correction, and placed in charge of all training programs on the same Rikers Island where Claude had spent a good portion of his life.

Chapter 25
On the Run

F airly soon after Tommy's birth, Pat conceived again, but this was not to be, as she miscarried in her third month. There would be many other miscarriages over the years and we would also suffer the loss of a stillborn daughter.

It is so difficult to write about this part of our lives because I know how painful it is for Pat, who, throughout this ordeal, was heroic and never lost the sweetness that is so much a part of her character and soul.

Life can sometimes rip you apart and this was the period that tried my soul. Just months before we suffered the loss of our daughter, my dad succumbed to his horrific two-year battle with lung cancer and died at the early age of 55. Right before his death, my mother—who was 49—suffered a massive stroke. Her physician told me that she would be dead in 24 hours, but my mother wasn't buying into that and she lived another 16 years, albeit she was never the same after she suffered the stroke.

I felt that my world was coming apart and I could do nothing to hold it together. I sensed that everything around me was spinning out of control, that nothing seemed to go right and that if anything could go wrong, it would. I wanted to escape and find a new way of living, where life was simpler and pain faded away into the distant past.

All of this pain occurring within such a short period of time was staggering, yet I didn't feel completely defeated—just worn out and hurt. I know that Pat's, and my faith got me through this period. And because Pat was always supporting me, I know that she did not have

the proper time to grieve the loss of our daughter.
Somehow, I think that Pat got lost in the shuffle during
this difficult period because people did not know how to
deal with a woman who had had a stillborn baby. Even
the hospital personnel demonstrated their ignorance
and insensitivity, by placing Pat in a room filled with
mothers who had just delivered healthy babies after she
had just lost ours. Today, a stillborn birth is treated with
the same respect and dignity as any other death. That
was not the case in the 1970s and it should have been.

The events of 1975 triggered a series of poor decisions
that had me seeking greener pastures and sprinting
away from reality, which I never imagined could be so
harsh.

Chapter 26
Greener Pastures

T he decade of the 1970's was a time when many Americans questioned the credibility of our government, became more disillusioned about society in general, and sought alternative ways to live their lives. Watergate divided our nation, but our government proved that the Constitution was alive and well, as the U.S. Supreme Court affirmed the principle that this nation was based on the rule of law and not the rule of man. Richard Nixon resigned the Presidency and Gerald Ford became the 38th President. Ford had replaced Spiro Agnew who had been driven from the Vice Presidency in disgrace. Events in our nation's capital dizzied Americans.

I had been promoted to a newly-created position that coordinated all the security and public safety services for the City University of New York's 20 colleges. Careerwise, all was well. But the strain from all my personal problems was affecting me in ways that I was oblivious to at the time.

Now in my mid-twenties, I was the senior executive in charge of public safety for a major university system. I was making good money; yet I was restless. I longed to get away from New York City, as if that would make everything right with my life.

I found some solace in my Catholic faith and even considered working for the Church in some capacity. Under the guise of searching, I was actually trying to escape from the horrors of the last year.

I had been teaching for four years at John Jay College of Criminal Justice as an Adjunct Assistant Professor and found it to be a fulfilling experience. I seemed to connect with my students and worked extremely hard, preparing lessons and developing innovative instructional techniques. In a way, I feared boring the kids, so I would use a variety of techniques, besides lecturing, to capture their attention. I found it liberating that I could do what I wanted in the classroom, that I did not have to get the approval of some bureaucrat before initiating new teaching techniques.

Students energized me and I found that when I was in the classroom I blocked out the stresses of life for the time being. Teaching reminded me of those carefree days on the baseball diamond, when my only worry involved trying to hit a nasty curveball, which I didn't do all that well. Throw me a fastball and I'd take you deep. Throw me a slow curve and I looked like a blind man trying to swat flies. But now, life was throwing bean balls at me and the only thing I could think to do was to bail out and run from them.

While the classroom provided a temporary barrier from the harsh reality of family illness, I never perceived it as a vehicle to shield my students from the realities of the hardball aspects of the criminal justice system. My job was to prepare these young people for careers in which they, too, would see horrible things, so they needed to hear about and study these issues. But in doing so, I did not want them to become hardened and cynical, so my lectures and class discussions emphasized the importance of living by a set of ideals.

Teaching restored my hope for the future; it was an environment for intellectual and moral growth for me—and I hoped for my students also.

I started to think that life would be more stable and happier if we were to move out of the metropolitan New York area and settle into a teaching job in some small town—the kind of idyllic place you read about in books. I visited colleges in Vermont and New Jersey and finally settled on the State University of New York at Utica. I liked the area (I didn't visit it in the winter) and thought the college's approach to criminal justice education was progressive and its curriculum cutting-edge.

The college made a job offer with a salary considerably less than what I was making as an executive at City University. After some weeks of soul-searching, Pat and I decided to head off to a full-time teaching position, which I had idealized as the perfect solution to our problems. We put our Long Island house on the market and sold it in two days. It was all so impulsive, but I figured that this formula had worked for us when we decided to get married and that it would succeed again. But I was dead wrong!

We bought a restored house with a wraparound porch in a small village right outside of Utica and enjoyed the summer in the Mohawk Valley. My mom had moved in with my grandmother and was recuperating rather well from her stroke. I worried about leaving them at this time but my strong-willed grandmother assured me that she could handle things. I wasn't really that far away from them—about a four-hour drive—and they would be visiting frequently. After I moved, however, I felt guilty about moving so soon after my dad's death. But I was a man on the run, driven by escapism, with my thoughts clouded by my desire for new beginnings where life would be better—as if New York City had anything at all to do with my problems.

I thoroughly enjoyed teaching at the State University, which was located across the street from the Utica Brewery and housed in an old mill in the center of economically challenged Utica—a city that had seen better days and was experiencing population loss just about every year. Since this branch of the State University was an upper division college, we had only juniors and seniors enrolled in our program.

Our house became a hangout for a number of these kids who were away from home for the first time and needed a hot meal from time to time. Pat and I were just a few years older than these kids, so I think they perceived us more as big brother and big sister than parent figures.

The school and the kids were great, but the weather was more than we bargained for. You would think that I would not have been surprised by the severity of the weather since we were moving into New York's renowned snow belt, but I guess I just blocked that out when I visited the college during the summer. Another smart move on my part.

But the weather was only part of the problem. For some unknown reason, Tommy became extremely sensitive to some allergens that triggered all-night coughing, which ultimately turned into asthmatic bronchitis. We went from doctor to doctor with no success. Finally, we noticed that his hearing had become impaired, so we got in our car and headed back to the Big Apple where Tommy had his adenoids removed and had Eustachian tubes placed in his ears. We also located a superb allergist in Brooklyn who cared for Tommy for the next twenty years. Pat and Tommy never returned to Utica.

I commuted on weekends throughout the entire spring semester; life was not easy during this time. But Tommy was under terrific medical care and he could now hear and was able to sleep through the night without those terrible fits of coughing.

I returned to Utica to complete the semester and sell the house that we lived in for less than two years. Then I had to find a job back in the metropolitan New York area and find a place to live, because Pat and Tommy were living with Pat's grandparents in cramped quarters in the Park Slope section of Brooklyn. Things were topsy-turvy, to say the least.

Utica exposed me to rural law enforcement and to the hardball world of small city politics. One weekend my criminal justice students joined forces with the State Police, as they conducted a thorough search of a crime scene, after a serial killer taunted police with hints that his victims were buried in this thickly wooded area. Nothing was found except some animal bones, but I had my first ride in a police helicopter as we scanned the search site from the air.

There was also the day that I was offered the position of Commissioner of Public Safety by the Mayor of Utica who had heard "good things" about me from one of his aides, who happened to be one of my students. I was smart enough to decline this invitation because the Mayor was embroiled in a very public fracas with the Police Chief and I wanted no part of that unstable situation. There was no way I was getting in the middle of this internecine battle between this eccentric mayor and the city's longtime police chief.

One battle I did get into the middle of, involved two faculty colleagues who got into a physical confrontation that, unfortunately, I walked right into one day. One professor was on this other guy's back pounding him with punches. The whole affair resembled either a mock rodeo or some slow-motion wrestling match. The profs bounced off walls and started to attract a lot of attention. At a point when I thought they would crash through the wall into a classroom filled with students, I moved in to break it up. I managed to separate the combatants, but the whole debacle wound up in Utica Criminal Court. It eventually got resolved as cooler heads prevailed.

When I wasn't acting as a referee, I found time to establish the Center for Rural and Urban Crime Studies at the college, as a vehicle to assist local criminal justice agencies in developing effective training programs. I delivered a course at the Utica Police Department, which was aimed at helping officers pass civil service promotion exams. I also ran a seminar for criminal justice personnel to train them in state-of-the-art techniques used in investigating sexual assaults, an innovative program that received local press coverage. I appeared on local television discussing a new program mandated by the State of New York for those who were convicted of drunk driving offenses. Utica, unlike the Big Apple, was a small media outlet, so programs of this nature got widespread television coverage in the Mohawk Valley.

My monograph titled, *Police Robbery Control,* had been recently published by the National Institute for Law Enforcement and the local newspaper did a feature article on me and the publication, which I had co-authored with my friend and colleague from John Jay College, Dr. Dick Ward. I became fairly well known in the area; I was now a big stone in a small pond.

But, my quest to escape life's problems ended as I bade my students and colleagues farewell and headed back to the town that just two years before I had fled in pursuit of greener pastures.

Chapter 27
Back Home

I spent most of the summer working at John Jay College writing grant proposals, an art I had learned from Dick Ward who offered me a summer position, as I sought to figure out what direction my career should now take. Dick would soon leave John Jay to become Vice Chancellor of the University of Illinois at Chicago Circle, where he would develop an international reputation in criminal justice academic circles. Dick is now Dean of the School of Criminal Justice at Sam Houston State College.

At a criminal justice conference held in the spring at Utica, I had met a senior administrator from New York Institute of Technology, who asked if I would consider joining his staff to revamp the college's criminal justice program. I knew little about NYIT's program, but I liked the idea that the college was located on Long Island and that, as part of my deal, I would receive a full scholarship to pursue a doctorate in public administration from Nova University, a progressive college in Fort Lauderdale that was a sister school to NYIT. I had been accepted into doctoral programs at New York University and Fordham University before heading off to Utica. Nova was an innovative institution way ahead of its time and had developed a number of doctoral programs designed for working professionals. I would be able to take a number of courses at NYIT, which would reduce my traveling back and forth to the main campus in Florida.

Dick Ward encouraged me to pursue a full-time faculty position at John Jay, but I had this sense that I had been there and done that, and that I really needed

to move on from my *alma mater*, which had treated me
so well over the years. I wanted to continue the journey
that got detoured in Utica, so I decided to take the NYIT
faculty position.

Pat and I and Tommy got in our car and went out to
Long Island where we put a binder on a modest, brick
ranch-style house with three bedrooms. Finally, the
three of us would be united under one roof and be a
family again.

NYIT proved to be the right decision at the right
time. I re-engineered the undergraduate curriculum and
immersed myself in the doctoral program, which required a major time commitment. I was exposed to a
superb faculty who literally trained me to think
differently about the pressing problems confronting our
cities and our nation. Studying public administration
provided me with a different set of conceptual lenses to
explore a variety of public policy and organizational
issues outside of criminal justice. I could sense that I
was growing professionally and that my interests were
now considerably broader, and my insights and written
commentaries were more thoughtful and sophisticated.

I completed the doctoral program in three years and
was now "Dr. Ward." I was elated, not so much by the
title (which I had to admit was a bit heady for a college
dropout from Brooklyn), but that the ordeal was over. As
much as I knew that, I now viewed the world differently
as a result of my doctoral studies. I was delighted that it
was all over because there was always lurking out there
the great fear of failure—that I would fail the comprehensive exam, that I would not get through the orals,
that something would go wrong and I'd fall on my face.
But I hadn't failed and now things began to move
quickly, even before the ink on my diploma was dry.

A month after receiving my doctorate I had the good
fortune to be introduced to Peter J. Brennan, a former

U.S. Secretary of Labor, who was seeking an executive director to run the New York State Committee for Jobs and Energy Independence, a nonprofit labor/management coalition he had established in the immediate wake of America's energy crisis of the 1970s. I interviewed with Secretary Brennan who seemed overly impressed by the fact that I had served in TPF. I could sense that the interview was going well, and it didn't hurt that Peter Brennan lived in Massapequa, my new hometown, and that his son-in-law was a New York City cop. I admitted right out front that I knew little about energy policy, but Brennan said that he needed a strong administrator and that he had consultants for the substantive issues. Besides that, he said I appeared to be a "quick study" and before long I would know more than "some of the pretentious fools who have credentials beyond their intelligence." Brennan, who didn't mince words, then pointed out that I had been a member of a number of unions and evidently understood the economic concerns of working men and women. I did little talking during the interview and was a bit in awe of this man who had come from New York's renowned "Hell's Kitchen" area of Manhattan all the way to the Cabinet of the United States. As I got up to leave the interview, Brennan said, "If you have the mettle to be in TPF, this is not going to be a problem for you. When can you start?"

Chapter 28
Mr. Secretary

P eter J. Brennan was an American success story, not in the sense that he became a wealthy and famous man, but more in the way that he had—as the saying goes—"pulled himself up by his bootstraps," to become a respected national labor leader.

Pete grew up in a cold-water flat on Manhattan's West Side, the area commonly referred to as "Hell's Kitchen." A tough, Irish Catholic who served on a submarine tender in World War II, Brennan was a painter by trade who rose through the union ranks to attract the attention of President Richard M. Nixon who appreciated Brennan's outspoken support for our troops in Vietnam. In the early 70s, Brennan led a widely publicized and controversial parade in Manhattan to demonstrate the construction unions' support for our troops in Southeast Asia. Elected to a second term, the Republican Nixon reached out to Brennan, a lifelong Democrat, and appointed him the nation's 13th Secretary of Labor. Admirals would now salute the sailor from the poor side of town.

While in Washington, a place he labeled the "City of Illusions," Pete witnessed the financial distress wreaked upon the American public by OPEC oil sheiks who, at their whim, could affect the international economy by manipulating the supply and price of crude oil. During the Watergate scandal, Brennan served on a Cabinet Council that was charged with exploring alternative means of energy, while monitoring the crisis that had millions of Americans waiting on long lines to get gasoline for their automobiles.

After Nixon resigned in disgrace, President Gerald Ford was advised to select his own Cabinet and Peter Brennan was offered the Ambassadorship to Ireland, which he declined, to the surprise of Ford and many of Brennan's friends who thought he was a perfect fit for that prestigious but largely ceremonial position. As Pete described it, "I heard from everyone I knew and hundreds of others I had never heard of, who all wanted to visit me at the Ambassador's House in Ireland. With all these freeloaders planning on visiting me, I would have been broke in six months. I couldn't afford that job even if I wanted it—and I didn't."

Brennan decided to return to New York where he resumed his position as President of the New York State Building and Construction Trades Council (AFL-CIO), which was a politically powerful association that represented New York's hardhats in Albany, at City Hall and in Washington, D.C. Pete now had a lot of political juice and the mention of his name opened up doors. Leaders in the business community respected him because the plainspoken Brennan was viewed as a pragmatist and not an ideologue; he called the shots the way he saw them.

Pete Brennan had a charismatic and suave demeanor that belied his streetwise and down-to-earth approach to defending the interests of America's working men and women. He would be equally at ease with Presidents and Kings and Queens and with laborers at construction sites. But he always preferred to be with the latter. He also had no use for so-called labor leaders who betrayed the trust of their members by using their offices for personal gain, or who became disconnected from the rank and file.

Pete Brennan did not suffer fools gladly. He could identify a phony from a mile away and he would dismiss him before the fool could get a word in edgewise with the loquacious Brennan, who knew the art of filibustering better than some of the Senate's best. No one told better, more amusing—or longer—"war stories" than Pete Brennan, the raconteur *par excellence.*

Working for Pete was as democratic and participatory an experience than I could ever imagine. Now armed with my new doctorate in public administration, I was conversant with the latest management theories floating around academe and government and corporate America. Brennan was as progressive and cutting-edge as it got. He managed by gut and intuition, and his approach focused on reaching a goal with the full support of his fellow workers. He encouraged and motivated people and, above all, he respected human beings and never perceived them as a means to an end. He never rode herd over people; he let them run freely with the full knowledge that he was there to support them. Brennan knew how to delegate authority; he believed in selecting the best people and then letting them do their jobs as they saw fit. I doubt he ever read a book on management; he never had to because he thought most of them were "horse shit." Amusingly, he called his approach to leadership "horse sense."

When Pete returned to New York in 1975, he convened a meeting of leaders from organized labor, the business community and government to explore the possibility of establishing a nonprofit organization with a singular and well-defined role—to make America energy independent. Brennan had found it abhorrent that OPEC could bring America to its knees by closing the spigots that controlled the oil supplies flowing from the Middle East. Pete saw this as a clear threat to our national security. As a consequence, Brennan believed that our lack of a rational energy plan jeopardized our

cherished and hard-fought freedoms. Brennan framed
the issue as one of patriotism, but he did it in a way that
the public policy issue of energy independence united
even those who were historic adversaries. Brennan's
brilliance in finding common ground amongst enemies is
legend and is an endangered skill in today's polarized
world. Out of this 1975 meeting came the proposal to
establish the New York State Committee for Jobs and
Energy Independence, which became known as JEI, and
Peter Brennan became its Chairman and President.

In 1980, I became JEI's Executive Director, having
succeeded Political Science Professor Robert Searby who
recommended me for this post when he accepted the appointment as Deputy Under Secretary for International
Affairs in the U.S. Department of Labor. I was now the
CEO of the largest and most powerful labor/business
coalition in New York State. This was quite different
from TPF, as I used to say to Pete, who quickly retorted
that at least in TPF you usually knew who the bad guys
were. "When they all wear suits, they're not that easily
distinguishable in the world of white-collar crime,"
quipped the sagacious Brennan.

I spent seven years with JEI and even got promoted
to the post of President, which Secretary Brennan
relinquished in order to get me more money. The job
exceeded all my expectations and I learned a great deal
about energy policies—or perhaps the lack of rational
ones—and about the politics of organized labor.

Our Board of Directors included CEOs and other
senior executives from business and leaders from the
labor unions. We established offices in the State Capital
at Albany, in New York City and on Long Island.
Regional committees were established across New York
State and our grassroots approach caught the attention
of lawmakers throughout the Empire State and in
Washington, D.C.

I learned the details of running a nonprofit organization, and I had a superb mentor in Pete Brennan who helped me learn the ropes of the public affairs business. Without a doubt, Pete Brennan was JEI; there could be no JEI without the leadership and name recognition of this former Cabinet Member.

I learned the ways of Washington, D.C., and quickly understood what Pete meant when he described it as The City of Illusions. This a town where power is the currency and where bootlicking by unctuous sycophants is state-of-the-art. The City on the Potomac and its architecture and history can give you goose pimples, but some of the people who work in this town have little or no concern for the public interest.

JEI taught me that there is a pressing need for more young people to get involved in public service. That is a hard sell, but it is a goal that is worth pursuing. Our future leaders are chasing dot-com fortunes and wasting their talents on accumulating wealth when their talents could be better used creating a more just and safer and fairer society. But who can blame them for not rushing to the challenge? The game of taking down our leaders has become fashionable. So why would bright and talented people want to enter public service where their imperfections will be investigated, magnified and reported with full gusto on the evening news? Who needs that? The risks are great and it is perceived that the rewards are minimal. So we are left with those who, by default, take on the reins of leadership and then they don't lead—they follow the path of least resistance. They are, for the most part, bankrupt of ideas for making America a better place for our grandchildren.

I also learned that I would never want any part of elected office and the life that went along with it. I was much too independent to listen to some pompous political party boss tell me how I should vote on a bill, much too impatient to deal with phony lobbyists, and still too idealistic to think that this is the way it all has to be done. Besides that, I still had a meteoric temper that could not be described as a political asset.

I perceived JEI to be an organizational model where diverse interests could iron out their differences with the common goal of serving the public interest. A foolhardy perception? Perhaps. But it made for an interesting and unique experience that I would not trade for any other opportunity. JEI became an exemplar in conflict management in the public policy field. The criminal justice system today could certainly benefit from such an enlightened and effective approach to conflict management.

It was during this time that I became a fairly accomplished speechwriter, primarily for Peter Brennan who, on one occasion, needed a speech because his long-time writer simply blew a deadline and failed to get Pete a draft on time. I asked Pete if I could take a shot at it. Pete liked my work, fired the highly compensated but unreliable speechwriter, and told me I could have the job if I wanted it. Speechwriting is an art. And speechwriters are powerful behind-the-scenes players, for they help shape public policy by proposing new and exciting ideas.

Over the years, I have written speeches for business and labor leaders and agency commissioners.

===

Ever one to find his way into the middle of a story—and an international one at that—I attended a speech by President Ronald Reagan at The Washington Hilton on March 30, 1981. Immediately after delivering his speech to an audience filled with union leaders, President Reagan was shot as he approached his waiting limousine.

I had managed to get a good spot to listen to the speech—I actually stood no more than 25 feet from the President's lectern. I even struck up a conversation with one of the Secret Service Agents on the protection detail. As the President left the stage, I started to make my way to the back of the ballroom when someone said that a Washington, D.C. cop had been shot outside the hotel. Then someone else said that a Secret Service Agent had been shot.

By the time I reached the lobby outside the ballroom, Frank Reynolds of ABC News was reporting that James Brady, Press Secretary to President Reagan, had been shot and killed. Reynolds quickly corrected himself and yelled at his staff, "Get it right."

There was a buzz that permeated the hotel and you could sense that you were at the scene of something big, something dramatic and tragic. Yet there was no definitive word on what had happened. I decided to make my way up to the main lobby where I tried to get to a phone to call Pat and let her know that I was all right. As I approached a bank of phones, I could hear members of the media yelling details into the receiver—so-called "facts"—that even I knew were still unknown or unclear about the entire situation. One guy got into a shoving match with another fellow and before you knew it one of the reporters got conked in the head with a telephone receiver.

I decided to go outside the hotel and strolled over to an area that was bordered on one side by a stone wall. This was the crime scene, but at this point it had not been sealed off. There was a splattering of blood atop a grating on a sidewalk drain. Later I would find out that it was Jim Brady's blood; he had been shot in the head.

Finally, it was reported that our President had also been shot; the impact of that thought was numbing. This amiable man, who had been in office less than three months, was fighting for his life at George Washington Hospital. I finally got to a phone and called Pat, who cried out of joy that I was safe, and out of sadness for the President and those who had also fallen at the hands of this deranged shooter.

I sat in my hotel room later that night and pondered the enormity of the assassination attempt. I just couldn't wait to catch the morning air shuttle to New York—and I hate to fly. I had tickets for Amtrak's Metroliner, but I was getting home as quickly as possible. I missed Pat and Tommy.

The President had survived surgery and even cracked some jokes along the way. The Great Communicator signaled that he was all right, that America was strong and the sun would rise tomorrow. Reagan did not want us to lose hope in the promise of America.

The television news showed clips of the shooting over and over again. The nattily dressed, personable African-American Secret Service Agent I had chatted with right before the President's speech, was now on the tube wrestling the crazed shooter, John Hinckley, to the ground. What a difference a few seconds can make!

I closed my eyes and waited for the sun to rise.

Chapter 29
Colossal Mistake

===

A s Pete Brennan prepared to retire, I jumped at the first job offer that came my way. This turned out to be a colossal mistake. I neglected to follow my own advice: Never make a job decision based on money alone, if you can help it. Don't follow the bucks; do what you love to do, do it better than anyone else, and the bucks will follow. The JEI coalition stayed around for over a decade addressing the energy crisis. But the coalition's continued usefulness was now being questioned by some of its members because America was putting energy policy on the back burner again. People no longer complained about long gas lines, and OPEC was staying within the boundaries of what was perceived to be acceptable oil prices. So our message started to sound like we were crying wolf again. Why worry about tomorrow? Actually, JEI was never needed more, but the urgency of the 1970s was becoming a faint memory for many, so it was time to move on and find something else to do with my life.

During my tenure at JEI, I had never positioned myself where I would slip into a job with one of our members or contributors when the day came that the coalition would fold its tent and disappear. I really didn't want to work for any of these companies or labor unions and felt that my next move would be outside the energy business, perhaps back to the criminal justice system or to another nonprofit association. JEI would remain stable as long as Pete Brennan was in the picture, but I knew that once he retired the contributors would disappear.

I was now known as Pete Brennan's right-hand man, but I did not have the political capital and name identification needed to keep the coalition alive as a powerful force in New York State politics. I was a good and loyal number two guy, but no one was going to rally around me and keep JEI going, particularly when hardly anyone gave a damn about energy policy. Union members were working and there was an adequate supply of energy available. At least until the next time OPEC decided to destabilize the world economy and demonstrate the power of the oil cartel. And there would be a next time; it was only a matter of time. (In the spring of 2001, gasoline prices reached and exceeded $2.00 per gallon.)

Pete Brennan still had contacts, but his political power was waning and little came out of his efforts to help me transition into something else. As the saying goes, "Once you're out, you're out." As Pete used to joke, people would approach him and ask, "Hey, didn't you used to be somebody?"

As JEI approached its final days, my good buddy Tom Creelman called one day and we arranged to meet for lunch at Long Island's Garden City Hotel. Tom's dad had been a legendary detective commander in the NYPD and his grandfather won the Congressional Medal of Honor for his heroic actions during the sinking of the U.S.S. Maine. Like his dad and grandfather, Tom has brass balls. In the early 1970s Tom had been one of my campus security officers when he was an undergraduate at John Jay College. He is someone I respect and trust fully. Tom is the brother I never had.

Tom now worked as a special investigator for a large health care company where he conducted and supervised fraud investigations. Prior to this job, he worked for the New York State Attorney General's Office as an investigator. Besides being a superbly talented and creative investigator, Tom Creelman is one of the finest human beings I have ever met. He is a standup guy, the type of loyal and reliable partner you would want to be with in a foxhole. Before long, we would find ourselves on just such a metaphorical battlefield, fighting a large and powerful corporate entity.

During lunch I told Tom that I would like to get back into the criminal justice field. Tom smiled. Then he told me that his organization was looking to hire a director for its fraud department and that I would be a perfect fit. The director would be the chief investigator and run the unit, which had about 40 investigators and support personnel. (I had managed to keep abreast of the literature and latest developments in the criminal justice field, by teaching as an adjunct professor during my tenure at JEI.)

Two weeks later I met with a corporate vice president who called me within days of the interview to offer me the job.

My gut told me to let this offer pass, so I turned it down. A month later I second-guessed myself and decided to reopen negotiations for the job, which I accepted after agreeing to a signing bonus.

The first few years of the job were gratifying and I liked the idea of nailing those bastards who ripped off the health care system. I reorganized the unit and decided that these white-collar criminals needed to be exposed to the criminal justice system and not be permitted to just make restitution and get on with their lives. A juvenile who is foolish enough to shoplift, and is apprehended, is arrested and held accountable for his or her misdeeds. So why are adults who commit serious frauds allowed to get on with their lives without experiencing the consequences of our legal system? Not anymore. Not on my watch.

This would be my policy. If you rip off the health care system, this is what you can expect to receive: First, we have you collared by either the NYPD, the district attorneys' offices or the feds, depending on the type of case it was. Second, we publicize your arrest so that it will serve as a deterrent to other knuckleheads who want to engage in similar conduct. Third, we get the money back by either a restitution agreement that becomes part of a plea deal, or we sue you in civil court. And, finally, if you are a medical practitioner who committed fraud, we go after your license with the objective of having it revoked or suspended by the State of New York. I called this the *"grand slam approach"*— and it worked like a charm. It felt good to be back working within the criminal justice system.

My unit became well respected in the field and we worked closely with the FBI, the U.S. Postal Inspectors, the various district attorneys' offices in the metropolitan New York area, and the NYPD in investigating health care fraud.

But then the vice president who hired me resigned and a new crew arrived who knew little about fraud investigations, but out of their collective ignorance they decided to micro-manage a successful fraud unit and demoralize it.

Before long, the corporation was under the gun from government regulators who were conducting a full-scale audit and review of the company's overall operations.

I essentially served as the corporation's Inspector General in that I was responsible for making recommendations to improve the company's internal controls and for investigating employee dishonesty, which made us the Internal Affairs Unit. Furthermore, the corporation held the Medicare contract and my unit had a reporting responsibility to the Health Care Financing Administration of the U.S. Department of Human Services. This arrangement gave us a quasi-governmental investigative duties, albeit in a limited way.

I felt that in order to do this job well I had to have some degree of independence, within, of course, the parameters set by senior management. It was important for my unit to call the shots, as we saw them, pending review by both the corporation's law department and the prosecutors. I wanted our unit to have "checks and balances" and accountability, so I put in place a Case Management Committee to review our investigative techniques and recommendations for handling fraud cases.

For a number of years, I had warned senior management that the company had serious internal control deficiencies that facilitated the commission of fraud. This message and my call for advanced technology and more investigative staff fell on deaf ears. Some executives chose to ignore or conceal the problems; they didn't seem to have the courage and leadership needed to correct them.

Finally, with the public in an uproar over astronomically rising insurance premiums, the state regulators and a U.S. Senate investigating committee looked into the company's mismanagement and its failure to address significant fraud problems. Prior to the arrival of the government's auditors and investigators, I had the feeling that nothing would ever be done about fraud because it was easier to pass the losses on to the already burdened consumers by increasing their insurance premiums. Is it any wonder why health care remains a pressing public policy and economic issue?

I had gained some name recognition in the health care field because of our successful investigative efforts and as a result of my many appearances on radio and television discussing the burgeoning problem of health care fraud. I held press conferences in Albany and in

Washington, D.C., and gave numerous speeches and workshops aimed at educating consumers on how to protect themselves from unscrupulous health care providers. I had even lectured on the topic of health care fraud at the FBI Academy in Quantico, Virginia. But I could not get senior management to direct its attention toward a problem that was pervasive and systemic.

Just about everyone knew where I stood on the issue, so I doubt there was much surprise when I was subpoenaed by the U.S. Senate's Permanent Subcommittee on Investigations, which was interested in hearing my views on the fraud problem. On July 19, 1993, *The New York Times* reported that I had "repeatedly battled with top company executives who appeared intent on closing their eyes to the fraud problem." The reporter culled his information from my deposition taken by the Senate Permanent Subcommittee on Investigations, which included the following testimony: "I have seen for six years the same types of frauds and inadequate internal control. It is urgent that this thing be turned around quickly."

The investigators were particularly interested in a fraud case that we investigated that involved almost $30 million in losses as a result of the company's inadequate claims system. The investigation involved the use of dummy corporations set up to get health insurance for seriously ill foreigners who came to the United States for expensive operations and then returned home. The dummy corporations listed these people as employees, and the health insurer never verified the existence of the companies or recognized that these patients, who kept coming on and off their health insurance policies in rapid succession, were citizens of another country.

This case represented the best example of how ineffective the fraud controls were in this beleaguered corporation. Corporate empty suits did not think in terms of justice; if it were up to them, white-collar criminals could just return the money they stole and get on with their lives. In that way, the crooks would get immunity and no-interest loans, to boot. That is not justice. Crooks wearing stethoscopes and expensive suits and using computers to commit their frauds should be collared and made to appear before the bar of justice.

This well-publicized international fraud case eventually made its way into civil court where two men were ordered to pay the health insurer $82.3 million after a federal judge found that they had engaged in a massive international fraud. As to whether the company received a single dollar of this amount, I doubt it. So the bottom line is: the company pursues the civil court remedy and winds up with two judgement-proof defendants who neither pay a red cent in restitution nor do they spend a single minute in jail. I guess that's corporate justice; it's certainly not criminal justice! The crooks should have been arrested in the first place.

I hasten to add that if anyone ever decides to go up against a large and powerful organization, then they better be ready for a rough and rocky ride and be prepared to pay the price. I retained personal counsel throughout this ordeal and the company had to pay my legal costs because I was acting within the scope of my corporate responsibilities by identifying the problems and simply telling the truth. But there is a price to pay for that.

I developed hypertension and other symptoms related to occupational stress. I became more cynical about the corporate culture and even about government, which I believe, in the end, was more interested in getting favorable press coverage than bringing about needed structural and policy changes in the health care industry. The fraud case quickly became yesterday's news and the government ran off to its next press conference.

About a year later I returned to public service. I left the private sector on my own terms, with my integrity intact, and I left with the knowledge that the vast majority of employees at this corporation were decent and hardworking people who were trapped in an organization with corporate policies that were not consonant with the company's public mission, which was to deliver affordable health care insurance in an efficient manner.

Throughout this ordeal, Tom Creelman stood tall and never wavered, for he comes from that long line of loyal and courageous forefathers. Tom Creelman is the real deal. Tom also decided it was time to return to public service and rejoined the New York State Attorney General's Office, where he now serves as a senior investigator. He is also an adjunct professor of criminal justice at St. John's University.

In 1994, I was appointed Assistant Commissioner for Training and Organizational Development at the New York City Department of Correction. I left the private investigations sector disillusioned, but enlightened by some serious lessons that I would share with the next generation of leaders when I finally returned to the classroom. But first, a long-term dream was to be realized; I was becoming a commissioner for the City of New York—not in the NYPD—but in the largest jail system in the world. Who would have thought?

Chapter 30
The Commish

M ayor Rudolph Giuliani campaigned on a promise to reduce crime and enhance the quality of life for all New Yorkers. The voters bought his pitch and David Dinkins, New York's first African-American Mayor, was sent packing after the 1993 election. One of Giuliani's first major appointments, and perhaps the most important one he would make, would be Police Commissioner. The Mayor selected William Bratton who had demonstrated creative leadership by reducing subway crime when he served as New York City's Transit Police Chief in the early 1990s. Bratton had left New York to return to his hometown of Boston where he was serving as Police Commissioner, but the chance to lead the nation's largest police department was enough for Bratton to leave Bean Town and head back to the Big Apple. He had reduced crime in the subway system and had a history of turning around inefficient departments; now Bill Bratton would have a chance to use his strategies above ground and across the entire City of New York.

The city welcomed this Bostonian with open arms; New Yorkers were fed up with crime and an aggressive approach would be applauded. Bratton, a man with a healthy ego not unlike his boss, boasted in his Bostonian accent that he would take back the streets of New York—one by one. He put together a team that did just that in a turnaround that led to a veritable revolution in policing around the globe.

But there was another component of the criminal justice system that also demanded immediate attention—the correctional system, which is often neglected by elected officials who believe that the bucks are better spent by putting more cops on the street. Police presence and effectiveness can be turned into votes, while correctional reform is a yawner for the public. Who cares about criminals and jails? Why spend money on a system that has not worked and shows little potential for change?

But Giuliani knew that the state of the jail system was not good, and while the inmates were not yet running the jails a case could be made that the entire system sorely lacked management accountability. So Giuliani tapped Anthony Schembri, the progressive Police Commissioner of Rye, New York, as his Correction Commissioner. Schembri, who had previously served in the Correction Department as its Deputy Inspector General, had developed a reputation as an innovative police leader, particularly in the area of domestic violence.

I had known Tony Schembri from my days at John Jay College, but hadn't seen him in over twenty years. I always liked Tony, a down-to-earth, energetic guy who had earned a law degree from Pace University while serving as Rye's Police Commissioner. Tony had been the model for the successful television program *The Commish* and still served as technical advisor for the show. He had come a long way from his days as an investigator in the Brooklyn D.A.'s Office. Tony had also headed the criminal justice program at Brooklyn's St. Francis College during the 1970s and was known for his unorthodox approach for promoting higher education for law enforcement personnel. Schembri liked to think "outside the box," as he put it.

During the summer of 1977, when I was trying to relocate to the Metropolitan New York area from Utica, I had a job writing grant proposals at John Jay College's Criminal Justice Center. One miserably hot, sticky day in July, I drove over to the college from Brooklyn to pick up my paycheck. I parked my Plymouth a block from the college, picked up the check and headed back to my car, only to find that it was missing. I had evidently misread the parking sign and my car had been towed to a pier on the west side of Manhattan. With about five bucks in my pocket, which is more than I usually had, and the banks already closed, there was no way I could retrieve my car, which would cost me $95. I stood on the street corner perspiring profusely and trying to figure out my next move. A few profanities passed my lips as I stood staring at the sign that I had managed to misread in my haste to park near the college. The sign could not have been any clearer; I had screwed up and most of my consultant fee would now go towards paying the fine and towing fee.

But then, lo and behold, around the corner walks the effervescent Tony Schembri, who volunteered to drive me to the pound and even gave me the cash to get the car released. The next day I mailed Tony a check with a thank you note. But we never got together again until he invited me down to the Commissioner's Office, after I had sent him a congratulatory note in which I wrote that if there is anything I can do to help him in his new job, that he could count on me. Attached to the note was a copy of my resumé.

Tony rushed over and gave me a big hug when I entered his spacious office, which was adorned with numerous awards and mementos from his career and his international travels. Within two minutes of our conversation, he offered me the job of Assistant Commissioner for Training and Organizational Development, a position he indicated would report directly to him because of his interest in "making the Correction Academy the premier training facility in the world." Tony indicated that I had the ideal credentials for this job and that together we would use the Correction Academy as the platform to change the culture of the organization. Tony told me to think about the offer, which I did for a split second and then I blurted out, "When do I start?"

I was now back in public service and out of the private sector. And I left on my own terms for something I truly wanted. I had become a commissioner and attained a lifelong goal that I harbored from the time I raised my hand and took the oath of office for the NYPD.

Tony told me that I would have to be interviewed by the Mayor's Chief of Staff before the New York City Department of Investigation would conduct my background investigation. I left Tony's office and walked over to the agency's Personnel Department, where I picked up a ton of forms that had to be filled out. I also called the Office of the Mayor's Chief of Staff and arranged an interview for the following week. Things were on a roll.

I met with Randy Mastro, the Mayor's Chief of Staff, the following week. As I walked into his office, Randy gave me a warm welcome and told me that I had the job if I wanted it. Randy had been the lead attorney on the RICO case involving the international fraud I had investigated and said he was impressed with my work and that I was exactly the type of person the Giuliani Administration wanted to attract to government service. The entire interview took five minutes, with Randy asking me one question: Did I have any philosophical problems or differences with the Giuliani Administration? I had none and I told Randy that I thought the Mayor had an opportunity to do great things for the City of New York. I truly believed that he could and would, and it is quite clear that Mayor Giuliani has led the City of New York to new heights. Even his most ardent opponents and detractors have to agree that Giuliani has been a successful mayor, particularly in the area of public safety. As we all do, Rudy has his shortcomings, but he made me believe that New York City could be managed. Up until this point, I didn't believe that to be the case, but Mayor Giuliani has made a believer out of me and a lot of others.

With the distinguished Churchillian leadership he demonstrated in the wake of the September 11th terrorist attack, I would not be surprised if Rudy Giuliani someday set his sights on the White House. Once President George W. Bush leaves office, *America's Mayor* may take a shot at becoming our nation's *Commander-in-Chief.*

I was impressed with the fact that the Giuliani Administration would permit the agency heads to select their management team from outsiders who had no political connections to the Mayor or his campaign. I hadn't come from any political clubhouse, and I had not made a contribution to the Mayor's campaign war chest. I had gotten the job because I knew Tony Schembri as an acquaintance over twenty years ago and I had the professional and academic background needed for this position. I suppose it didn't hurt that Randy Mastro knew of my work, but that had really nothing to do with my initial selection. I would be a political appointment in the sense of the word that I was not covered by Civil Service protection; I could be fired at any time for any reason, or no reason, whatsoever. That goes with the territory in this type of job. I would serve at the pleasure of the Commissioner; I knew that coming in, and was willing to accept that condition of employment, for that's the way it works in high-level appointed positions—and it makes sense.

My background investigation took a few months to process and then I finally got the call to report to the Correction Academy in Middle Village, Queens, on July 12, 1994, for my swearing-in by The Commish, Tony Schembri. I arrived early and put the final touches on my brief remarks, which I would make after Tony handed me my gold commissioner's shield and administered the oath of office. I was a bit nervous but determined to take command of the situation. I delivered the remarks without notes and didn't miss a beat, and I could see that my message was well received by the audience and by Tony, my new boss. As I left the room, the uniformed members saluted me and I have to admit that this acknowledgment of my rank felt terrific. I was now Assistant Commissioner Ward, and I liked the sound of that title, for it fit just fine.

After the ceremony, I went to Rikers Island with Tony, who introduced me to some members of the senior staff. I had not been to Rikers Island in years and, while I didn't visit any of the island's ten jails that day, I could sense an air of depression and gloom, which affects me every single time I travel over the bridge that connects Queens with this penal colony of hopelessness.

Later in the day as I drove home, I held the shiny gold shield in my hand and smiled all the way home. It was the same smile I sported back in 1969 when I received my silver police officer's shield and my TPF collar brass. The years had passed, yet my enthusiasm and idealism were the same.

Chapter 31
Bernie Kerik

T he agency grapevine had it that most of my colleagues on the senior executive staff thought that I was a close personal friend of Commissioner Schembri, that we went back many years together and even socialized together. This rumor got around the department and I could sense that I had acquired quite a bit of political juice in short order. It didn't hurt that I was a direct report to the Commissioner, which was an arrangement that Schembri wanted and ordered. Up until that time, the Assistant Commissioner for Training and Organizational Development reported to a Deputy Commissioner, so this organizational change was big news and subject to the rumor mill and agency grapevine.

I decided not to disabuse anyone of the notion that Schembri and I were close friends because it would obviously help the Correction Academy get the resources it needed to become the standard of excellence in correctional training. I had instant access to the Commissioner, but I didn't abuse it. In fact, I had to hold Tony Schembri off at times because he is a man with a million ideas and he wants to implement all of them at once. Tony had to make an adjustment from running a relatively small police department to being the CEO of a large and complicated agency with 10,000 uniformed staff, 1,500 civilians and a budget exceeding $750 million.

Tony attracts attention because he has a dynamic personality fueled by unending enthusiasm and a never-say-no type of attitude. But he was attracting the type of negative media attention that was making it difficult for him to begin the process that was needed to transform this tradition-bound and inefficient agency into a well managed and more performance-oriented department. The unions were battling with Tony as he tried to reduce overtime and make managers more accountable for the performance of their subordinates. There were also staff members who remembered Tony's days as the Deputy Inspector General when he aggressively investigated allegations of corruption against department employees and, of course, made a few enemies. That went with the territory. Tony would tell people that he no longer wore the "black hat of the IG," that he now wore a "white hat" and his job was to motivate and lead the entire agency. He stated that he was a "coach" and wanted all his managers to think of themselves as coaches charged with leading winning teams. Tony's enthusiasm was infectious, but he couldn't get out of the starter's gate because of bad press that seemingly always had The Commish on the ropes defending himself. Finally, after only ten months on the job Tony resigned because, as he put it, he didn't want to be away from his family who remained in Westchester County while Tony lived in the City because of a residency requirement. Other versions had it that Tony was forced to resign by the Mayor.

I was on my way to an ophthalmologist when the Commissioner's Office beeped me; the signal 911 meant that something big was going down. I called Tony on my cell phone and he told me that he had resigned and he didn't want me to hear it on the news. I was stunned. I had been in the job just six months and now figured that I, too, would have to resign. I just couldn't believe that this was happening, yet I wasn't totally surprised because the move to get Tony out was becoming a juggernaut that seemed to have as its only outcome his resignation from office. The press had labeled him "Hollywood Schembri," and now the media had a field day with the news of his resignation. I felt bad for Tony who loved this position and sincerely wanted to improve conditions for both the staff and the inmates. But that was not to be. Now I wondered if my strategy of letting people think that we were close friends would come back to haunt me.

The following day I went to headquarters, which was located at 60 Hudson Street in lower Manhattan, with the hope of seeing Bernie Kerik, the new First Deputy Commissioner who had been Tony's Executive Assistant. Bernie Kerik and I started around the same time at Correction and, while we didn't know each other all that well, we hit it off right away, probably because both of us had served in the NYPD. Bernie was a highly decorated detective who was on leave from the Police Department and I could tell that he was a talented and hardworking guy. I spotted Bernie in the hallway and asked if I could see him for a moment. He could see that I was troubled, so we went to his small office outside the Commissioner's suite and he closed the door.

"Bernie, I'm going to resign and let the new Commissioner have the opportunity to select his own guy," I said to Bernie. Kerik looked me straight in the eye and said: "Are you nuts? You're not going anywhere. You're doing a good job and you haven't made any enemies. Just stay put and do your job. Everything will be all right," Kerik stated as he pointed his finger at me to emphasize his point. "The new Commissioner, Mike Jacobson, is a good guy and you're staying here. You got it?" Kerik again pointed his finger at me. But I could see that Bernie was troubled and conflicted. He had developed a close working relationship with Schembri and now Tony was gone and the Mayor had chosen Bernie for the critically important number two spot in the agency. Bernie was saddened by Tony's departure but simultaneously ecstatic that Mayor Giuliani had enough confidence in him to tap him for the post of First Dep. I also noticed that Bernie's demeanor radiated a sense that he was in charge and he would eliminate any obstacles that got in his way. There was something about this guy that made me feel comfortable, and certain that he was a lot more than a Detective on leave from the NYPD, who was now in this executive position because of his political contacts. There was a whole lot going on here and I sensed that Bernie Kerik wanted to prove that he was up to the task, that he wanted to prove that those who whispered that he'd last no longer than six months were dead wrong.

Kerik had a unique background. He had been the warden of the Passaic County Jail in New Jersey before he decided that he would hand in his gold shield and head to New York City as a rookie cop at the age of 30. He had also spent four years in Saudi Arabia as a security specialist with the Royal Family after serving in the U.S. Army. He held two black belts in the martial arts. This was no ordinary guy. Bernie Kerik had natural leadership ability and he was a quick study. Kerik didn't have the word failure in his vocabulary. He had presence and could be intimidating; he also didn't suffer fools all that well—or at all. (In August of 2000, Mayor Giuliani would name Bernie Kerik the 40th Police Commissioner of the City of New York.)

The new Acting Commissioner was Michael Jacobson, who would also remain as Probation Commissioner, as he reluctantly took on the reins of power at the Department of Correction. Jacobson is by far the brightest and most self-effacing person I have ever met in government service. This low-profile and experienced administrator, who had served in both the Koch and Dinkins Administrations, was the perfect appointment for our beleaguered agency. He held a Ph.D. in Sociology from the City University of New York and had sort of an understated professorial way about him.

Mike Jacobson called a senior staff meeting his first day on the job, and allayed the fears of the assembled commissioners and uniformed chiefs that a wholesale change in personnel was in the works. As the unpretentious Jacobson spoke, you could sense that this guy had a special gift, that Mayor Giuliani had selected the right guy to get Correction on the right track, and that he would do it without creating the dislocation that often accompanied sudden organizational changes.

The tandem of Jacobson and Kerik would transform the Department of Correction at a pace faster than that of the NYPD, where the radical transformation of the police department became an international success story.

Chapter 32
In Command

T he New York City Department of Correction in 1994 was a resource-deprived agency that suffered from poor employee morale, which was triggered by heightened inmate violence and mandatory overtime. Discipline was lacking in this quasi-military organization, the appearance of the uniformed staff was dismal and sick leave was reaching astronomically high levels. New recruits had not been hired in five years, which forced the existing staff of approximately 10,000 correction officers to work excessive overtime, with the dangerous result that some correction officers were suffering from burnout.

Arguably, correction is one of the most challenging and least attractive positions in the criminal justice system. Correction officers are constantly under stress; they deal with the most violent and difficult people on this planet and it is not unusual that a correction officer would be slashed, assaulted or have feces and urine thrown at him or her. I have tremendous respect for correction officers and the job they do—as do most police officers who readily admit that they would never want to work in a jail or a prison.

When you think of it, how many people do you know who desire careers in corrections? Many of the people who accept these jobs do so out of financial necessity or by default—somehow things just worked out that the correction system called them from a civil service list and there is nothing else available in the job market, so they decide to give it a shot. Or, they are related to someone in the system and decide to follow the relative's or friend's footsteps and become a legacy, as we call it in corrections. It seems odd to me that in an organization that suffers from such chronic poor morale that there would be so many young people following in the footsteps of parents and siblings and other relatives.

I took over a training academy that needed to have its curriculum re-engineered and its organization re-designed. My predecessor in this position had done a fine job and was well respected, but he had not had the opportunity to train newly appointed officers. Frankly, the lifeblood of an academy flows from its recruit training school. A special energy flows in a training academy when recruits are present; the rookies provide the faculty with an opportunity to present state-of-the-art curriculum for training probationary correction officers, and they encourage the staff to present a professional image to these new members of the department.

I reviewed the curriculum that had been used in the recruit school over five years ago and junked most of it. The courses were stale and the length of the program—7 weeks—was ridiculously short by any standard. How do you train someone to become a professional correction officer in 7 weeks? And one of those weeks is actually in a jail for field training. It takes longer to become a barber in New York State, for heaven's sake. I discussed this with Commissioner Jacobson who, on the spot, agreed with me and told me I could double the training. Jacobson, besides being brilliant, is gutsy and was willing to fight tooth and nail with the City's Office of Management and Budget to get the necessary funds to increase this training. But first he had to convince the Mayor that we needed recruits now.

Jacobson developed a financial model that presented a compelling argument that the City could actually hire new officers within the existing budget, by using over-time dollars to fund recruits who would reduce the spiraling overtime once they finished training and hit the jails. The recruits, Jacobson argued, would earn less than veteran officers forced to work overtime at time and a half. His model also demonstrated that the disbenefits associated with mandatory overtime included increased sick leave for burned-out officers and the potential of law suits resulting from excessive use of force incidents that stemmed from officer fatigue and poor morale.

Jacobson had to convince a wary Mayor Giuliani that the agency needed additional personnel because Giuliani wondered why Los Angeles, which had approximately the same inmate population of New York, could operate with about half the uniformed personnel. It took some time, but finally the persuasive and steadfast Dr. Jacobson convinced the Mayor that we did not want to run the City jail system in the same manner that L.A. ran theirs. According to Jacobson and Kerik, the L.A. jail system had excessive violence and inadequate staffing levels. At last, New York would hire correction officers and they would receive the re-engineered curriculum, which I used as my vehicle to let the Academy staff know that I was going to do things my way—and not their old way.

When I first introduced the idea of offering a new curriculum, I sensed that there was resistance on the part of some staff members who seemingly felt they had to defend past practices. They had missed the boat entirely. If they didn't catch up with it at the next port then they were not going to be a part of the "new" Academy crew. It was not my intention to disparage past practices; it was my job to make this the finest training academy in the field and I was going to do this with them or without them. They were either going to be part of the team or they were going to be shipped back to jail service, if they were uniformed personnel. Civilians, who could not support my changes, were also going to be transferred or reassigned to positions where their negative attitudes wouldn't get in the way of my progress.

My message was loud and clear: buy in to progress or get out. I was not about to tolerate obstructionists.

As a part of my reform package, I reorganized the Academy into four academic disciplines and appointed chairpersons for each of these new departments. Academy instructors would now become specialists in their areas as opposed to jack-of-all-trades generalists. I established a task force to re-engineer the entire recruit program and then set about doing the same thing for our in-service training program. Finally, I created a *Leadership Institute* for middle and senior-level managers and personally taught its first course, which was on the topic of executive decision-making.

I had the full backing of Commissioner Jacobson and First Deputy Commissioner Kerik, both of whom took a special interest in supporting the Academy and its new initiatives. Along with Eric Taylor, who was Chief of Department and the agency's highest ranking uniformed member, Jacobson and Kerik put in place a management accountability system that would revolutionize corrections, much the same as the vaunted COMPSTAT System had transformed the NYPD into an efficient and effective crime-fighting organization. The new executive staff at Correction was getting its signature on an agency that had long resisted new ideas and fought off previous management attempts to change the culture of this mammoth agency that now has an 860-million-dollar budget.

It's important for a leader to earn the respect of the troops, so I knew that I would have to do that in order to accomplish the ambitious goals I had set for the Correction Academy. I worked long hours and sometimes would arrive at 6:30 A.M. to make an impression on the staff and get a good start on the day.

I attended roll calls and addressed the uniformed and civilian staff frequently. I sought the staff's input and tried to improve working conditions and provide incentives for those who went the extra mile in doing their jobs.

I didn't tolerate chronic lateness or excessive sick leave. If an officer had a personal or family problem that needed attention, I did all I could to make sure that I supported him or her through those tough times. I tried to be approachable and friendly, while making sure that I kept the proper distance that befitted my rank.

I believed that I should practice what I preached, so I made sure that I did not miss work on that Monday in January of 1996 when a blizzard paralyzed the City of New York. This happened to be the day that 365 recruits were to report to the Correction Academy for their first day in uniform. There was no way I would miss this event. I figured the message should get out to both staff and the recruits that if the Assistant Commissioner can make it to work during a blizzard then they, also, should make every effort to do so.

It was clear to me on Sunday that this was going to be a major storm, so I called Captain Tony Lodato, my Director of Administrative Services; we both headed to the Correction Academy as the snow started to fall. A local Italian restaurant remained open Sunday evening and as we ate our pasta and drank a little red wine, we watched cars slide down a hilly street that ran next to an already snowcapped cemetery. It was clear that we were headed into a disastrous storm.

After dinner we made our way back to the Academy, where we tried to get some shuteye as the mice ran freely throughout the facility. We caught little sleep, but we earned the respect of the 100 recruits and staff who managed to make their way through the horrendous blizzard that just about closed down the entire East Coast of the nation.

Without doubt, my prior experience as a member of the NYPD helped me establish a rapport with the uniformed members of this agency. I also developed a close working relationship with the heads of the unions of the uniformed ranks and gained their trust and respect.

One of my most memorable experiences in Correction was when Norman Seabrook, the President of the Correction Officers' Benevolent Association (COBA), presented me with an award plaque at a recruit graduation at Brooklyn College, which was attended by Mayor Giuliani. I had no idea that this was to occur and my colleagues said I looked stunned. But this was Norman's very public way of saying thanks to me for implementing a training program that he felt enhanced the academic, physical and firearms skills of the new correction officers who were joining the ranks of the department. This plaque is prominently displayed in my den at home, along with another one that declares that I am an Honorary Correction Captain, an honor bestowed on me by Peter Meringolo, the President of the Captain's union, when I retired from the Department of Correction. On an adjacent wall in my den hangs a Certificate of Distinguished Service awarded to me by Commissioner Mike Jacobson for my "distinguished leadership of the Correction Academy." And on my desk lies my gold Assistant Commissioner's shield, which was presented to me by Mike Jacobson and Bernie Kerik when I left office and accepted a faculty appointment at St. John's University. I don't mean to sound immodest, but I am damn proud of these awards.

I also have to believe that Peter Brennan, the man who taught me everything I know about labor/management cooperation, would have been proud of his protégé.

The best speech I ever drafted was my eulogy for Peter Brennan. It was the most difficult speech to deliver, but an easy one to write because it was driven by pure emotion and wonderful memories. I got through it—although there were some tough moments—and everyone in the crowded church stood and applauded Secretary Brennan for the patriot and leader and great man that he was. It was my finest speech, but the one I dreaded to deliver for it was my final farewell to my mentor and good friend.

Chapter 33
Cycle of Despair

T here are few new ideas circulating in correctional administration and few leaders willing to take the risk of doing something bold and creative when it comes to inmate programs. As a society, we are essentially doing the same thing with prisoners that we did a hundred years ago; we're warehousing them until we release most of them back into society where a good percentage of them will be re-arrested and incarcerated once again.

We understand this cycle of despair; what we don't understand is how to break it and release ex-offenders who are drug-free, prepared to be gainfully employed, and committed to civic values that reject their past behaviors and embrace a crime-free lifestyle. Sounds good. But there is no magic formula or public policy elixir that can bring this about because human behavior is too unpredictable. Furthermore, we as a society are unwilling to experiment with anything that could in any way be categorized as liberal, fuzzy and soft on crime. So we continue the thoughtless practice of warehousing and releasing and then re-incarcerating again. Our communities suffer every time we unload another busload of ex-offenders back into neighborhoods ill-prepared to deal with these ex-convicts.

Jennifer Wynn in her recently released book, *Inside Rikers,* paints a bleak picture of the recidivism issue:

> "Every year, approximately half a million people in the United States leave correctional facilities and return to society. Every *day*, approximately 350 ex-offenders return

to New York City from prison or jail. The
majority will be back behind bars within
three years of their release."

And because there is no real public support for
developing innovative rehabilitation programs, leaders
in corrections have been disinclined to experiment and
possibly hurt their careers by proposing something that
is perceived as not "being tough on crime." Except for
some academicians who seek progressive solutions to
criminality—but often lack the institutional experience
and political savvy to transform their ideas into viable
experiments—there is little energy directed toward
changing the warehouse approach. Where you have little
experimentation, you have very little progress. As such,
the *status quo* continues to reign supreme on these
islands of hopelessness—our nation's jails and prisons.

When some states spend more on correction than they
do on education, we should be asking some hard questions about our priorities.

Somewhere in America's prisons is a recidivist who
will take a life when he's released. Maybe we need to
think of this problem from a selfish perspective. Maybe
we need to look through a new set of conceptual lenses
that provide an entirely different view of the problem.
Perhaps we better start *thinking* about crime and not
just reacting to it in a knee-jerk fashion.

There will always be crime and victims. But that does
not relieve us of the obligation to explore new ideas and
develop viable programs that will improve public safety
by doing something fundamentally different in our jails
and prisons. As is always the case when promoting new
programs, the devil will be in the details and in the
closed minds of those who seek to embrace the past and
its decades of failures.

Dennis Hawkins, a career prosecutor, and now an adjunct professor at St. John's University, puts it quite well: "I have spent my entire professional life putting people in jail. Now I want to give some thought to finding better ways of protecting our communities when these people come out. The present system is a failure and in the end our communities suffer the most. This is not justice when unrehabilitated ex-cons are released to communities that are totally unprepared for their release. No one is served by this policy."

We have done remarkably well in improving the management of our jails and prisons. In New York City, the Total Efficiency Accountability Management System (TEAMS) has transformed the nation's jail system into one that is better organized, less violent and consistent with the tenets of sound public administration. The agency runs extremely well and Mike Jacobson and Bernie Kerik deserve full credit for this organizational revolution that has been acknowledged by Harvard's John F. Kennedy School as an innovative approach to management accountability.

Violence in New York City's jails has been reduced by 94% since 1994, which is a remarkable feat that has been covered by *60 Minutes* and featured in two *Court TV* documentaries, among others. The New York City Department of Correction's Gang Intelligence Unit is considered the finest in the correctional field; the members of this elite unit are widely respected throughout the criminal justice field. The current Correction Commissioner, Bill Fraser, is a career veteran of the department who has built upon the success of his predecessors and added his special brand of leadership to make this department an exemplar in the area of violence reduction and overall correctional management.

In Jennifer Wynn's thoughtful book, *Inside Rikers,* Anthony Smith, the head of the New York City Horticultural Society, which is the group that runs a greenhouse program for Rikers prisoners, states: "Michael Jacobson was a truly extraordinary commissioner. He really cared about inmates not coming back." Jacobson is also credited with adding almost 1,500 additional beds for drug treatment on Rikers Island. Jacobson did this in a jail system where the average stay for felony offenders is only 140 days, and the recidivism rate is around 75%.

But now we have to turn our attention to the issue of inmate programs throughout the American correctional system, particularly in prisons where offenders are sentenced to at least one year of incarceration. Put simply, we must find a way to convert warehousing into the actual correction or transformation of human beings. And when we do, we will all fare better as a result.

No longer can this issue be reduced to an irreconcilable battle between political philosophies and ideologies. It's time to throw away the counterfeit justifications for continuing the *status quo*. Now is the time to be bold in our thoughts and deeds.

Many of the vicious criminals now held in our nation's jails and prisons are beyond rehabilitation, and I have absolutely no objection to keeping them incarcerated until they're carried out in a pine box. In fact, I demand it! These predators deserve to be behind bars and must be kept there. But what about those inmates who will inevitably return to their communities and, for a variety of reasons, will commit more crimes against us? From a selfish perspective, I want to enhance public safety by taking a hard look at the warehousing issue. Without doubt, the vast majority of the 2 million people now held in our nation's jails and prisons will return to our communities some day. And when they do, will it be the same old story again? Well, we just had them stored away in a warehouse until such time as they were released, to once again inflict their harm on society.

Dennis Hawkins got it right; "Let's look at this problem from a selfish perspective this time." Maybe it's time that more public policies are viewed from such a "selfish" perspective. What do we have to lose? Perhaps we have something significant to gain. We can, and must, break this cycle of despair!

Chapter 34
The Professoriate

A former Cabinet Secretary once said, "It's time to leave government, so I can have time to think about the most pressing issues facing our country." It was now time for me to leave government service and return to academe, where I could think about some of the most pressing issues facing the criminal justice system. I had accomplished what I wanted to at the New York City Department of Correction and decided it was time to embark on the final leg of my professional journey, one that I hoped would be my most productive and longest.

My trek would continue with my acceptance of a senior faculty position at St. John's University, where I would head the university's Criminal Justice Program and serve as a consultant to both police and correctional agencies. I would now reflect on my professional life and share my thoughts and ideas with my students in my role as a professor, and with my colleagues in the practitioner world as a researcher, writer and consultant. It was a logical next step and a fitting close to my practitioner life.

It was during my first year at the Department of Correction that I received a call from Professor Craig Collins of St. John's University inquiring about the possibility of arranging a field trip to Rikers Island for a group of undergraduate criminal justice majors. Craig Collins, a retired sergeant from the NYPD and a national expert on gangs, was a legendary figure at St. John's who, over the course of twenty years, quietly built the Criminal Justice Program into the largest and most successful undergraduate program at the university.

Craig was a no-nonsense guy singularly devoted to his students. Legend even has it that on Christmas Day he would be in his office for a few hours knocking out recommendations to graduate schools for his "kids."

Craig could be testy at times and he hated the bureaucratic aspects of higher education, but he loved the classroom and understood the influence that he could have on his kids, most of whom were first generation college students. And he certainly influenced his "kids," such as Ed Norris who now serves as Baltimore's Police Commissioner, and Christopher Rising, an attorney, who served as chief speechwriter and Special Assistant to New York City's Police Commissioner Bernie Kerik; and Dr. James O'Keefe, the former Director of Training for the NYPD who is now a colleague of mine at St. John's University. The old sergeant certainly left his mark.

I arranged the field trip for Craig's kids and addressed the group before they anxiously departed the Correction Academy for their trip to Rikers Island. After I gave my brief comments, Craig pulled me aside and asked if I would be interested in joining the adjunct faculty at St. John's. I told him I would be honored to do so, but that I would have to limit myself to one night a week because of my hectic and somewhat unpredictable schedule. Craig said that was no problem since evening courses met once a week for three hours at the Queens Campus, which was located just five miles from the Correction Academy.

Craig also invited me to give a guest lecture to the Criminal Justice Students' Association, which was attended by over two hundred students and faculty. My presentation, titled "Corrections: The Hidden and Forgotten Component of the Criminal Justice System," was well received by an audience that actually surprised me with a large number of questions. I felt comfortable at St. John's and the audience reaction was warm and generous, particularly when I told them that I had dropped out of St. John's when I was seventeen. There was nothing pretentious about the St. John's crowd; they made me feel right at home.

It was truly a special honor to be appointed to the adjunct faculty at the university from which I had unceremoniously dropped out thirty years before. In a way, I felt redeemed; I had now made this whole thing right and I believed my parents would have been proud that I finally returned to St. John's. Now the dropout was a member of the faculty. How ironic!

I taught a class on *American Correctional Systems* and knew immediately that, once I completed my mission at the Department of Correction, it was back into the classroom for my career finale. The classroom energized me; it was a forum where I could bridge the gap between theory and actual criminal justice practice, where war stories became case histories that students would hopefully remember and which could influence them during their careers. My classroom became my platform to encourage students to be thoughtful and question accepted beliefs and practices. I could encourage them to push the envelope and be inventive; I could challenge them to find ways to make our society safer and more just. And I could impress upon my students the necessity for ethical leadership in the criminal justice system and life in general.

On occasion, I would meet Professor Collins at the Faculty Club where we would discuss the latest rumors in the NYPD and the progress we were making at Correction in reducing violence in the jails and improving the quality of training for correctional personnel. Every single time Craig would ask if I could take another intern at the Department of Correction. And each time I would tell him to send me someone reliable, not one of his special projects who had never heard of such a thing as an alarm clock.

Craig was deeply and surprisingly interested in corrections and, on more than a few occasions, he would express his admiration for the men and women who worked the nation's largest jail system. He believed that it was a more demanding job than that of police officer and admitted that he found it difficult to encourage his kids to pursue careers in the correctional system. Craig saw all of these students as his grandkids—and treated them as such. He worried about them.

At our last luncheon together, Craig and I kicked around the idea of a master's degree program at St. John's. I shared my thoughts with him and he just smiled; he asked me to send him a memorandum outlining my ideas, which he said he would use "to make some of these academic eggheads understand what the field really needs." I could tell that he liked what I had to say and would put to good "political use" my observations on what I thought constituted a relevant and academically rigorous graduate degree.

It would be the last time I would speak to Craig, who had become a friend. Two weeks later, while grading term papers at his office at home, Craig suffered a massive heart attack and died doing what he loved to do—serving his students.

I attended Craig's memorial service at the university and was struck by the level of affection the kids had for their beloved professor. It was a touching tribute to the man who built the Criminal Justice Program from scratch and loved every minute of what he did. The kids seemed in a collective state of shock and, while I understood their sense of loss and even abandonment, I also felt a sense of joy that this generation would be so touched by a teacher five decades older than most of them. His passing even strengthened my belief in the idea that teaching is an extraordinary profession in which every class provides an opportunity to do some good for someone. The charismatic Craig Collins had done a lot of good, and his legacy lives on and sets the standard for those who have the unenviable task of following him in the professoriate.

Dr. Angelo Pisani, a colleague of Professor Collins, took on this unenviable task of running the Criminal Justice Program, which seemed to be in an institutional state of mourning unlike anything I had ever witnessed before in my professional life. We always hear that no one is indispensable and that all of us can be replaced in our jobs, but Craig's death tested that aphorism, as many students seemed to fall into a state of funk, for lack of a better term. To Angelo Pisani's credit, he led the program during these difficult days and during a time when he was a candidate for tenure, a difficult task that requires a single-minded dedication to scholarly responsibilities. Angelo, a former Deputy Commissioner in New York City's Department of Investigation as well as a former member of New York's Finest and Bravest— having served in both the NYPD and the City's Fire Department—navigated some difficult waters and stabilized a program that reeled after Craig's sudden death. His faculty colleagues rallied around him and the students came to understand that Craig's gift to them is timeless and their memories of—as some kids affection- ately called him—"the old man," could not be wrested from them by such a sudden passing of their beloved mentor.

A few months after Craig's death, Angelo Pisani and I met at the Faculty Club essentially to get to know one another. During dessert and coffee I casually mentioned to Angelo that I would be interested in returning to academe. Angelo mentioned that the university would be hiring two professors for the fall semester and indicated that he thought I would be a strong candidate. I applied and received a job offer after being interviewed by a Search Committee and the Dean of the College, Dr. Kathleen Vouté MacDonald, an upbeat and indefatigable administrator, who is now the senior Dean at the university.

Little did I know that I would shortly assume the leadership position that Craig Collins defined and held for over two decades at St. John's University. I would never have predicted this outcome.

Chapter 35
Rites of Passage

A month into my new career as an Associate Professor I assumed the position of Director of the Criminal Justice Program, the post that was shaped and defined by Professor Craig Collins and then ably served by Dr. Angelo Pisani, who decided that he would like to return to his full-time teaching responsibility and relinquish the directorship. Did I really want to take on this leadership responsibility? Frankly, I was conflicted. My strong desire to teach competed with this opportunity to lead a respected academic program at a major university in New York City. I left the Department of Correction to teach full-time at the university and, while I would still teach three courses per semester, I would now also be responsible for a variety of management tasks. I had been in leadership posts my entire adult life and now looked forward to teaching and writing. I had my fill of dealing with bureaucracies. Besides, I was joining an established faculty and was concerned that my colleagues would resent this outsider who would now have some supervisory responsibilities over them. These were the same faculty members who would vote on my reappointments and ultimate application for tenure. How could you supervise the same people who voted whether or not you still had your job? The organizational arrangement seemed odd and could conceivably put me in harm's way. The decision actually became moot, when I quickly realized that no one else wanted this job. I either took it, which would probably help me attain tenure if I didn't screw it up, or alienate my peers who would vote their displeasure, or I declined it and would disappoint the

Dean who wanted me to take on this leadership position. By default, so to speak, I became the Director before I even knew the names of all the faculty members in my department.

The position, however, was prestigious and widely respected in the New York criminal justice community, so I decided to make this work for St. John's University and for me.

Let me quickly add that my colleagues have been absolutely supportive of me and I have never felt that they viewed their votes as a coercive means to get me to follow their wishes or avoid my responsibilities. I work with a classy group of professionals and have tremendous respect for all of them. In fact, they define the word collegiality, which in some colleges is nothing more than an empty word.

A colleague of mine, Professor Giles Casaleggio—a former prosecutor who had also served as mayor of a municipality in New Jersey and is a member of my academic Division's Personnel and Budget Committee—later told me that he also felt it was somewhat bizarre that he would have to vote on recommending merit raises for "his boss," as he put it. So, in fairness, the organizational arrangement was not optimal for my colleagues either, but we made it work!

The able Chairman of the Division of Criminal Justice and Legal Studies is Bernie Helldorfer, a full professor who is an attorney, and does an exceptional job coaching St. John's nationally ranked Mock Trial Team. Bernie is my boss and he is a calming influence in an environment that sometimes, contrary to the media's portrayal of academe as serene and laid-back, can be hectic and occasionally filled with political intrigue. In our academic division, however, we not only get along and like one another, but we work extremely well as a team, which is quite unusual in academic circles where egos clash as a matter of course.

In 1999, the SJU Mock Trial Team earned the distinction of placing second at the national championship, beating a number of Ivy League colleges on the way to becoming the nation's runner-up. Bernie, along with another colleague, Professor Oscar Holt—a talented and creative trial attorney— did a superb job of coaching our kids and preparing these future lawyers for careers in our judicial system.

Students are the lifeblood of a university; the more diverse the population, the better the education process. St. John's prides itself on serving predominately first generation college kids and children of recent immigrants. This has always been an essential element of the St. John's mission and it makes SJU a special institution with a noble goal. I have learned so much from my students and I am intellectually and spiritually enriched by the wonderful stories they share in the classroom. A classroom of students from diverse ethnic, racial and religious backgrounds, creates a superb environment to discuss the most pressing issues facing urban policing. St. John's mirrors the metropolitan New York area; it provides a laboratory for tomorrow's leaders to explore new ways to make our society fairer and better than it is today.

Higher education challenges us to pursue—as the Ancient Greeks called it—the "good life," which is based on individual virtue and shared community values. College is not a four-year retreat from the real world; it is a vehicle for all of us to help shape a better world, where success is not defined and judged by material gains.

As is my leadership style, I waited to get the lay of the land before making changes and advancing suggestions that I thought would strengthen our program. My first semester was absolute hell: I had three new courses to prepare; I had to learn the job of director, attend numerous committee meetings and prepare the infamous Personnel Action Form—known as the PAF— which is essentially a monograph of your entire professional life that must be submitted to three different committees every year for reappointment, and then finally for tenure consideration. These committees decide if you have a job the following year, and if you receive the brass ring of teaching, which is tenure. The PAF is due in October. I had just started in September and now had to construct my entire professional and academic life and commit it to paper in a highly detailed and precise format.

I also took on the role of faculty moderator of the Criminal Justice Students' Association and started to draft an article on correctional management. At one point during "hell year," Pat said that she thought I had made a mistake taking this job, that I was working more hours than I did at the Department of Correction. I knew I had made the right decision, but I was frustrated. I now knew why no one wanted this position. This was not what I had bargained for and things had to change. I now had a better understanding of why Professor Craig Collins found it necessary to go to his office and do some work on Christmas morning.

Once I submitted the PAF, I suggested to my colleagues that it was time to re-engineer our undergraduate curriculum, which had been in place for many years and needed some fine-tuning. I also recommended a new core curriculum for our criminal justice program and my colleagues enthusiastically endorsed this idea. Professor Susan Lushing, a twenty-seven-year veteran at St. John's and a gifted attorney, worked on this initiative and produced a creditable revision that we introduced to our students the following academic year. Susan and Dr. Keith Carrington—a former police commander from Trinidad and Tobago—would lead a faculty committee that would re-engineer the criminal justice undergraduate curriculum and make it state-of-the-art.

I struggled through the first year and decided that something would have to give if I were to be successful from both a personal and university perspective. I immediately set out to make this position more efficient; I eliminated unneeded tasks and delegated others to some of my colleagues. I prioritized my duties and eliminated those that were unnecessary or should be abolished because of resource constraints. I took full command of the situation and then refocused my energies on the classroom and on writing articles that would strengthen my application for tenure. I found that the same principles of leadership that I used in the Department of Correction would be useful at St. John's, with the exception that my staff and colleagues didn't have to salute me. My direct orders now became subtle suggestions that were more fitting to academia. My transformation from commissioner of a quasi-military organization to professor was coming along, due to the untiring support of my understanding colleagues.

There had been discussions carried on over a period of two years between my colleagues and faculty members from the Sociology Department, about designing a graduate program in criminal justice. I applauded the idea but was wary of trying to carve out a curriculum between two different departments from two different colleges of the university. My colleagues and the members of the Sociology Department had two distinctly different visions of what the master's degree in criminal justice should be at St. John's. We favored an approach that linked theory with actual criminal justice practice and had as its primary focus management and leadership of the criminal justice system. The sociologists favored a more research-oriented degree that would prepare students for doctoral studies. Both proposals had merit, but a marriage was not in the works.

After numerous meetings and drafts of proposals, it was evident that, as Kipling put it, "never the twain shall meet." So we parted ways and I spent an entire summer drafting my vision of a graduate degree, one that would be well received by the practitioner world because it would prepare students in the art and science of criminal justice leadership. I called my new proposal, *"The Master of Professional Studies in Criminal Justice Leadership."* This would be the first of its kind in the nation. The proposal would be unanimously approved by all the governing bodies at St. John's and then would receive approval by the State Education Department within a week of its submission. I consider this accomplishment one of my most distinguished efforts because, frankly, it took vision, diplomacy and leadership to get this idea from paper to reality and it serves—and I hope this doesn't sound immodest—as a classic case study in institutional leadership. I am especially proud of this graduate program and now serve as its founding director. My vision of a graduate degree in leadership was unanimously supported by a group of senior executives who serve on our Criminal Justice Advisory Council. I had formed this council for the purpose of making sure our programs are relevant, state-of-the-art and meet the needs of the practitioner world. This graduate program, unlike many in the field, was not crafted in some ivory tower on a campus far removed from the streets and courts and prisons where criminal justice personnel serve the public. The program was designed in such a way that our graduate faculty didn't just lecture about arcane academic theories. Our professors had practiced what they now teach because all of them were former senior executives in the field who had earned doctorates. They had led before they taught and the practitioner world appreciated the fact that they had earned their stripes as both leaders and academicians. The pejorative notion that "those who can, do—and those who can't, teach," in no way applied to our Criminal Justice faculty.

For example, our course on *International Terrorism* is taught by Dr. Harvey Schlossberg, a clinical psychologist and former detective, who founded the NYPD's Hostage Negotiations Team and served as the Chief Psychologist at the Port Authority of New York and New Jersey, when terrorists first bombed the World Trade Center in 1993. Harvey and his staff at the World Trade Center treated the hundreds of men and women who were traumatized by this attack that killed six people and injured hundreds of others. The author of *Psychologist With a Gun,* Harvey is an internationally respected expert on terrorism and is widely quoted by the media. More importantly, he is a loyal friend and a devoted teacher who during his recent battle against cancer never missed a class or an appointment with a student. Always a cop, Harvey never fails to answer the call to duty. In the aftermath of the September 11, 2001 act of war that toppled the same World Trade Center and killed almost three thousand people, Harvey rushed to our campus and volunteered to assist any members of the St. John's community who felt they needed to talk to a counselor about the horrific events that forever changed America.

As another example of the practitioner/academician approach used in our Criminal Justice Program, Adjunct Professor Bill Gardella bridges the world of theory with professional practice in quite a unique way. Bill, who is a retired Deputy Inspector from the NYPD, has a special interest in the area of serial killers and delivers a lecture on this topic that leaves the audience spellbound. He is also the Detective Sergeant who drew his weapon and arrested David Berkowitz, the infamous *Son of Sam,* who was responsible for killing six people and terrifying millions of New Yorkers during the mid 1970s. Bill Gardella has done it—and he can teach it!

Chapter 36
The Brass Ring

T enure is the brass ring in the teaching profession. It generally takes six years to wend your way through the rites of passage, before a university will grant tenure to a professor. Because of my previous teaching experience, I would be a candidate in four years, which was more than enough time for me. The entire process can be stressful and frustrating at times.

Professor Sharon Norton, a former assistant district attorney who had earned tenure the year before and now serves as an associate dean, advised me on how to present my case to the various personnel committees. This counsel was extremely helpful and I felt prepared— yet apprehensive.

As I stated to the members of the University Personnel Committee who heard my case for tenure, "I have never worked harder than I have during the last four years." I wrote articles on criminal justice leadership; I attended and participated in professional conferences; I became active in professional societies and foundations; I took on extra committee work and additional assignments at the university and I served as the faculty moderator for the Criminal Justice Students' Association. More importantly, I worked extremely hard at becoming an excellent teacher and developed innovative instructional methods to better serve the students. And, of course, I developed and implemented our innovative graduate program in Criminal Justice Leadership. I also became St. John's ambassador to the criminal justice system and established an Advisory Council composed of well-known, senior executives in the field, including former New York City Police Commissioner Bernie Kerik and New York City Correction Commissioner Bill Fraser.

I may have sounded like I was blowing my own horn, but that is exactly what you need to do to earn tenure— and you better not hit the wrong notes or you'll be unemployed. While timidity doesn't bode particularly well when seeking tenure, bald-faced arrogance will get you nothing but the door if you can't meet the stringent requirements for tenure. Hard work, creativity, a sense of collegiality, excellence in teaching and research, and an abiding commitment to good scholarship and to the mission of the university, will punch your ticket and get you the prize. It also helps not to make enemies of committee members and other influential members of the university community. You may be an outstanding scholar, but if you have influential and powerful enemies then you are significantly reducing your chances for being granted tenure. It's just a fact of life in higher education. It's also a fact of life that if you do have quite a few enemies then perhaps you're lacking something when it comes to collegiality and should therefore not be granted tenure.

Before I entered the conference room where the personnel committee met, Professor Peter Cardalena took me for a walk to the chapel where we received ashes; it was Ash Wednesday. Peter is another good friend, a man who is revered by his students, and as funny a guy you could ever find on a college campus. Pete is another blue-collar professor; he's a retired Transit Police Lieutenant who worked his way through St. John's for his undergraduate degree and then went on to law school and admission to the bar. He's a man of great faith; he calls himself a "positive Christian," and he was my archangel on Ash Wednesday because I needed someone to take me for a walk at that precise time. The tension was building in me and the time spent in the chapel gave me serenity and brought a sense of proportionality and perspective to the whole affair. Pete told me he guaranteed that I would be granted tenure, and his confidence and good humor that morning became a godsend for me. Pete's optimism is contagious, and I now know why the kids think the world of him, for I feel the same way.

In my pursuit of tenure, I touched all the bases—twice, my wife would say—and earned tenure on February 28, 2001. I could not have been more ecstatic. Finally, the college dropout from Brooklyn was a member of the club—a tenured faculty member at the university I dropped out of 35 years before. A sense of relief and pure joy filled my being and I knew that the entire journey had been worth it. I love teaching at St. John's and now I knew that I could remain there for my entire professional life, which will be the last leg of my journey through the criminal justice system and the higher education profession.

My good friend and colleague, Dr. Karim Ismaili, hugged me and took me out to lunch right after the ebullient Dean MacDonald informed me that the personnel committee had voted 16 to zero to confer tenure. Karim is a gifted scholar from Canada who will have a long and distinguished career as an academician. He has all the right academic tools to make a name for himself in the field. Besides that, he's a great guy who has supported me all the way.

As Karim and I ate our lunch in the Sly Fox Inn, a St. John's hangout within short walking distance to the campus, we concluded that my taking on the director's post had made the journey toward tenure rougher than it had to be. But the rewards at the end were sweet indeed and I had no regrets whatsoever. Always one to seek leadership posts throughout my career, I had been somewhat reluctant to take this one on, but now I thoroughly enjoyed it and looked forward to continuing in this position. In the end it all worked out. Somehow it always seems to, and this notion further reinforces my belief that all things happen for a reason. In time and with patience and faith, we come to better understand some of life's unpredictable twists and turns.

Tenure is a misunderstood term and concept. While it brings with it job security, tenure provides a freedom to pursue scholarly pursuits that faculty members deem important to themselves and to the teaching profession. I will actually work harder now than I did before receiving tenure by virtue of the fact that I will immerse myself in scholarly and professional activities that prior to tenure I simply did not have the time to address. I will be more selective in what I choose to take on, and I'll work under stress that now is self-induced as opposed to the kind that is driven by the arduous tenure review process.

My personality is such that I would never perceive job security as a license to join the ranks of some professors and teachers across our nation who hide behind tenure as a shield for their incompetence, laziness and uncaring attitudes. That is not why I entered this noble profession. Tattered lecture notes and stale lectures will never be my standard in the classroom. My students will never get shortchanged.

The conferral of tenure brings with it an ethical obligation to continue to serve my students with diligence, enthusiasm and with absolute respect. I would expect no less of myself now that I am tenured. In fact, I now demand more of myself. With tenure comes an obligation to develop professionally as a teacher. I will always consider myself a work in progress.

There is still much work to be done. And I intend to stay—as Teddy Roosevelt said—"in the arena" where the action is and where I can make continuing contributions to the criminal justice system.

My role model is Dr. Alex Smith, *Professor Emeritus* at John Jay College of Criminal Justice, who at the age of 91 still knocks out scholarly articles and advises me—his former student—on how to navigate through the shoals of higher education. Alex Smith is a distinguished scholar and quintessential mentor; more importantly, he is my friend and one of the reasons I am a college professor. Alex is still in the arena and his advice to me over the years has been priceless.

It is my hope that as the years go by that I, too, will be remembered by some of my students as a mentor and lifelong friend. For that would be a wonderful way to end my journey!

Chapter 37
Bon Voyage

It has been an eventful journey; I have seen the elephant and even had to get out of his way at times. I have sometimes put myself in harm's way and luckily escaped. I have had tons of fun and played many roles in life. I have been one lucky son-of-a-gun. And I still find it hard to believe that the confused and immature kid who dropped out of college is now a professor at that same university! Only in America!

I have laughed and cried my way through this journey. And I know full well that I am still this work in progress who, I hope, in some small measure through this book, can help you as you take your first steps onto the metaphorical battlefields of the criminal justice adversarial system.

No longer do I have the long hair that I had during my undercover stint. Male pattern baldness took away that option. Today, I shave my head; it's far better than the comb-over. My weight, however, is the same as it was when I first donned my NYPD uniform, although my waist has expanded a couple of inches.

I think I may have mellowed somewhat and may even be more patient these days. And I am a step or two slower, so I no longer run after fleeing felons—if I can help it. Today, I am the proud grandfather of 2-year-old Emma, a blue-eyed, redheaded beauty who has wrapped me around her little finger. For some reason, redheads take a liking to me.

I look at the world differently than I did when I first hit the streets as a young and wide-eyed TPF cop. And I have come to know myself better. I am no longer the impulsive young man who wanted to conquer the entire world. The battles and war stories give a person a different perspective on life. So does maturity. I am at peace with my career, and myself.

Every port-of-call on this unpredictable and sometimes rough voyage positioned me to be where I am today. As I trace the circuitous path of my career, I now understand that I would not have returned to St. John's University if I had not touched all the bases along the way. Even the two years in the snowdrifts of central New York placed me in a position where I discovered that I was a teacher at heart. Things happen for a reason.

From a professional perspective, I am delighted that we have finally abandoned the misplaced notions of some criminologists that the police have little impact on crime. Yet, I am equally distressed that the rift between the police and the community may be as wide as ever. The revolutionary changes in crime fighting were long overdue; now we must complete the job and encourage a trusting partnership between the people and the police— and then crime will decrease even more.

As Chairman of the Police Commissioner's Board of Visitors, I hope to play a role in forging stronger bonds between New York City's diverse communities and the people who serve these neighborhoods as police officers. It's time for the cops and the kids, and their parents, to play a friendly game of stickball in the streets of our city.

Now that we know how to better manage our jails and prisons, the challenge will be to find ways to depopulate these human warehouses and still make crime go down. This complicated challenge must be addressed because a half million ex-offenders will be returning to our nation's communities every single year. It will be interesting to see how all this plays out and if some professor at St. John's University, a hundred years from now, is still lamenting our society's high recidivism rates. I hope that's not the case.

I am now more firmly convinced than ever that there is differential treatment of offenders in our nation. My experience with white-collar crime convinced me that Lady Justice is not so blind at all; she peeks from behind that blindfold and sometimes gives a crook a pass if he's white, wears an expensive business suit and owns a stock portfolio. Meanwhile the black shoplifter languishes on Rikers Island, unable to raise $500 bail. This is not justice!

There is always a pathway out of the wilderness and my journey sought that break of light. In the end, my search led me back to St. John's University, where the final chapter of my professional life will be written.

War Stories provided me with an opportunity to revisit my professional life and share its vicissitudes with you. It is my hope that my unorthodox career path, and its *War Stories*, can be instructive to you. If readers avoid the errors I made, then I would consider this book a triumph. If they learn something from my modest success, well, then, that's a bonus. As you experience your own war stories, be ever mindful that the best tales end peacefully and justly.

Godspeed and Bon Voyage!

Epilogue

T he world changed forever on September 11, 2001. As I looked out a window of my university office building and saw smoke billowing from the World Trade Center, it all seemed surreal. This could not be happening to America. Shortly afterwards, the second tower collapsed and thousands of our fellow Americans and hundreds of heroes perished.

During the anxious days that followed this cowardly attack, as we mourned our great loss, it struck me that the role of policing in our democratic society would be radically changed. It already has changed to the degree that the NYPD just recently appointed a Deputy Commissioner for Counter-Terrorism and a Deputy Commissioner for Intelligence. Both of these newly-created, senior-level positions signify that policing must now be full partners in a collaborative effort between local law enforcement and the federal government—including the military—in rooting out and destroying terrorist cells. Our freedom depends on accomplishing this objective.

As I wrote the first draft of this book during the summer of 2001, it never passed my mind that I would be writing an epilogue on the topic of terrorism. But our world changed dramatically and so did the role of the police service. It seems somewhat odd to call our nation's police officers *freedom fighters*, but that is exactly the role the brave men and women in blue must play, if we expect to preserve our right to live in a free and safe nation of laws and due process.

As New York City Police Commissioner Raymond Kelly stated recently, "We are a nation at war." Our nation's police will be on the front lines in this war against domestic crime and international terrorism. In the end, freedom and justice shall prevail!

Questions for Discussion: Food for Thought

INTROSPECTION

- To what extent do your childhood experiences contribute to your thoughts, ideas and philosophy regarding crime and justice?

- What are your reasons for pursuing a career in criminal justice?

- What factors and forces contributed to your decision to pursue a career in public service?

- Do you have a particular role model in the criminal justice field? How has he or she contributed to your career choice?

- What are your short-term and long-term career goals?

THE POLICE SERVICE

- In your opinion, can a police academy adequately prepare recruits for the "street?" Discuss your position on this issue.

- Must there be a gap between police training and actual police practice?

- Should a college education be required for police officers? Why? Why not?

- How would you strengthen police-community relations? What are some of the barriers that prevent an effective relationship between the police and your community?

- Is it ever proper for a police officer to accept a free meal from a local restaurant? What is your position on a police officer accepting a gratuity from a local merchant? What is your definition of police corruption?

- How can "police humor" help reduce an officer's stress level? When does humor *cross the line*—so to speak—and become counter-productive?

- What skills are needed in order to be an effective undercover operative?

- Why are police departments having such difficulty attracting applicants? How can this problem be resolved?

- Why does organized crime remain such a potent force in American society?

- What are the most pressing issues facing the police service in the 21st Century?

THE CORRECTIONAL SERVICE

- Would you consider a career in corrections? Why? Why not?

- What is your philosophy regarding corrections?

- What are the objectives of the American Correctional System?

    * Punishment?
    * Rehabilitation?
    * Restitution?
    * Deterrence?
    * Incapacitation?

- How can recidivism be reduced? What programs and strategies would you propose to accomplish this goal?

- What is the role of the contemporary correction officer?

- What skills are needed to be an effective correction officer?

- Should a college degree be required for correction officers? Why? Why not?

- What are the most pressing issues facing American Corrections in the 21st Century?

IN THE INTERESTS OF JUSTICE

- In your estimation, is there differential treatment of the offender in the criminal justice system? If so, is it based on race, gender, religion, economic status, or some other factors?

- Should white-collar criminals be treated differently by the criminal justice system? Explain your position.

- What harm does white-collar crime have on our society?

- Should corporations be required to report all white-collar crimes to criminal justice agencies, as opposed to treating these offenses as civil matters?

CRIMINAL JUSTICE LEADERSHIP

- Are individuals born as leaders? Or, can individuals be trained to become leaders?

- What are the characteristics of the successful leader in criminal justice administration?

- It is said that the difference between successful leaders and those who do not ultimately succeed, is the way in which individuals deal with failure. Do you agree with this premise?

- What are the most pressing leadership issues confronting the criminal justice system?

- In your estimation, what were the most important milestones in the author's life, and how did these help form his opinions and thoughts on crime and justice?

CRIMINAL JUSTICE EDUCATION

- Why are you pursuing a degree in criminal justice?

- What is the difference between professional training and criminal justice higher education?

- If you are already working in the criminal justice system, what are your career goals and your expectations from higher education?

- What qualities do you look for in a professor of criminal justice?

- Do you feel your criminal justice curriculum bridges the gap between theory and actual criminal justice practice?

- Are you prepared to deal with your own "war stories" as a criminal justice practitioner? How do you manage stress?

- How has *War Stories* affected you as a person and as a future criminal justice practitioner and leader?